ON COURT WITH THE SUPERSTARS OF THE NBA

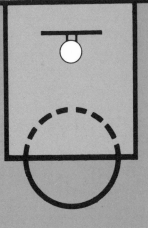

NBA
PLAYERS ASSOCIATION

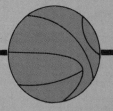

NATIONAL BASKETBALL
ASSOCIATION PLAYERS

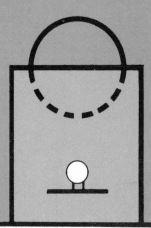

ON COURT WITH
THE SUPERSTARS
OF THE NBA

Edited and with an Introduction by
M E R V H A R R I S
in cooperation with the
National Basketball Players Association

The Viking Press / *New York*

*For Nancy, my sweetheart, helpmate,
critic, buddy, nurse, and love.
And a damned good editor, too.*

Acknowledgments

To gather the views of professional basketball's greatest players. on the fascinating complexities of their sport has been a project no man would dare attempt or possibly be able to complete without the contributions of many, many people. Larry Fleisher of New York, counsel for the National Basketball Players Association, Corlies Smith and Ray Ford of The Viking Press, and Chick Schmitman of General Licensing Corporation helped develop this book's concept and growth, and NBPA leaders such as Oscar Robertson, Dick Van Arsdale, John Havlicek, and others offered not only encouragement and assistance but also their considerable expertise.

The greatness of Elgin Baylor as an athlete and personality and the friendship and guidance of the late Louis R. Mohs, general manager of the Los Angeles Lakers for their first seven seasons in Southern California, were the major factors in my intense interest in pro basketball originally. The gifts of their time and advice by former coach, then general manager, Fred Schaus, broadcaster Chick Hearn, trainer Frank O'Neill, and stars Jerry West, Rudy LaRusso, Tom Hawkins, Wilt Chamberlain, Walt Hazzard (whose name now is Abdul Rahman), Jim King, and others through the seasons added greatly to my interest in and knowledge of the game, as well.

Other general managers, coaches, players, front-office members and the warm, selfless men who serve as NBA referees have been friends and educators for me too, and I would offer particular gratitude to Jack McMahon, Red Auerbach, Franklin Mieuli, Ben Kerner, Alex Hannum, Bill Sharman, Eddie Gottlieb, Johnny Kerr, Al Bianchi, Joe Mullaney, Sid Borgia, Mendy Rudolph, Richie Powers, Joe Gushue, John Vanak, Gus Johnson, Dave DeBusschere, Tom Meschery, Larry

Costello, K. C. Jones, Dick Barnett, Happy Hairston, Wayne Embry, Don Nelson, and many, many additional past and present NBA stars. Off-court, Pidge Burack, Marty Biegel, Ed Lieser, Len Corbosiero, Warren Turnbull, and Nick Hyman, among many friends of basketball, have been lavish with good advice and warmth.

Fellow basketball reporters and commentators Frank Deford, Bill Libby, Peter Carry, Joe Jares, Jeremiah Tax, Leonard Lewin, Leonard Koppett, Jack Kiser, Bill King, Hank Greenwald, Seymour Smith, Jim Schottelkotte, Johnny Most, Murray Janoff, Doug Ives, Haskell Cohen, Dan Hafner, Mike Morrow, Skip Carey, Mitch Chortkoff, Joe Gilmartin, Jim Murray, Mal Florence, and many, many others— in no particular order of listing—have freely offered advice and information and good company over the years, and I would thank them too. J. Walter Kennedy, a visionary and warm man, the depth of whose contribution to pro basketball may never be sufficiently recognized, has been generous not only with his personal friendship, but also with assistance in his office as commissioner of the NBA.

Finally, my thanks for providing the photographs used in this book to Nick Curran, director of public relations for the NBA, and to each team's individual publicist, with special appreciation to Jeff Temkin of the Lakers, John Steinmiller of the Bucks, and Frank Blauschild of the Knicks.

MERV HARRIS

Long Beach, California
October 1972

CONTENTS

ON COURT WITH THE SUPERSTARS OF THE NBA

INTRODUCTION:
IT ALL STARTED WITH
TWO PEACH BASKETS
AND THIRTEEN RULES

Jerry West, as pale and fragile-appearing as a boy playing among men, makes time stand still by bringing his team to victory with an impossibly long, impossibly launched jump shot in a frozen moment of athletic perfection.

Oscar Robertson demonstrates the human body's potential for grace and agility with flowing movements that seem effortless, but which less talented men dare not even attempt to duplicate.

Wilt Chamberlain, a bearded hulk of a man, unleashes the dark fury of man's repressed aggressions by the savage thrust of ball through hoop.

Willis Reed fights the agony of battle-inflicted injury to lead his team to glory both by deed and by inspiration.

These are elements that make professional basketball a captivating kaleidoscope—swirling, writhing, engrossing, thrilling. Light and shadow and fury and emotion attack the senses relentlessly. Huge men perform incredible feats of athletic skill in a compact area in which action and time are compressed and in which all participants and all spectators become involved. Even in the largest arenas, it is a game that can be heard—even smelled—not just observed casually. The sport is a reflection of the times in which we live. Events whir past at a pace that challenges comprehension, each new circumstance altering the process in which yesterday's truths become today's

Golden State Warrior Jeff Mullins gets some late help from teammates, but Milwaukee's Kareem Abdul-Jabbar has already begun his picture-perfect jump shot, taking advantage of a mis-match situation set up by Oscar Robertson and by Mullins' defensive switch.

uncertainties and today's hopes become tomorrow's ideals. Basket-ball, like life, begins with happy expectation: to become the best player in the community, to earn a high-school letter, to become a collegiate All-American, to become a star professional contributing to a championship team, to cheer, if you cannot play, for your team and your hero. Every opponent brings new challenges, and even in defeat there can be satisfaction that effort was made, and made with dedication and honor.

The astounding abilities of professional players, the intimacy with the game that even the largest arenas make possible, the pandemoniums in victory and the dejections in defeat have made professional basketball one of the nation's most popular sports. The ultimate skills of the NBA stars having excited the interest of youngsters, they seek in ever-increasing numbers to enjoy the game themselves in their playgrounds, schools, and recreation programs. The game cuts across lines of geography as well as lines of per-sonal wealth. It is enjoyed and followed by the corporation presi-dent as well as by the raggedy-clothed youngster of the mid-metropolis ghetto. It is enjoyed in the cities and on bare dirt courts in rural villages. Basketball is fun to play and to watch, and it is also a reflection of daily life in a compressed, showcased way which reminds its participants as well as its spectators that complete dedication to a goal is worthy of a man's best efforts, but that when the final whistle has blown, there is time to consider deeper values than merely the winning or losing of a game.

Professional basketball is a sport to be enjoyed at many levels. The youngster discovering the game for himself may visit the professional team arena and see his heroes execute easily and per-fectly plays he himself is struggling to perfect. The new fan sees the frenzy of the pro game, hears the grunts and shouts of the players, is captured by the raw excitement of what may appear to be a patternless, simple game. The more experienced viewer, aware of team-play concepts and other intricacies, enjoys his courtside hours more fully, even if not necessarily with more excitement. In this book, the attempt will be made to entertain the new as well as the long-time fan by discussing some of the seemingly endless aspects of the professional game. This is not a "how to" manual on fundamentals, but there will be information here that might help a young player master the sport's subtleties.

Of course, there is more to pro basketball than merely what

happens in a 48-minute game. Pro basketball is also a commercial enterprise—a successful one growing in popularity each year. The players are strong individualists with all the foibles and follies, ironies and problems of the human animal. Conflicts occur constantly among players, among executives, between front office and playing floor. Sports pages headline these problems in pro basketball these days almost as frequently as they do victories and defeats. Long, long articles reporting these off-court disputes are published by the news media and reported on radio and television because they may influence a team's success, and also because they are stories about flesh-and-blood people whose personalities fans have come to appreciate. This book will not delve deeply into this area of pro basketball, not to ignore it, but because a player's personality and problems are shaped by the game as it unfolds on the playing court.

The "people versus people" elements are for many the greatest fascination in the game. Long after game scores and high point totals are forgotten, it will still be possible to savor and reflect upon the whimsy of a Dick Barnett, the intensity of a Jerry West, the cool precision of an Oscar Robertson, the selflessness and relentlessness of Kareem Abdul-Jabbar. Yet, until the dynamics of the game are grasped, until the responsibilities and techniques of individual players are understood, it is difficult to enjoy fully the wonder of it all.

Here is an introduction and exposition. Here is how the NBA superstars play basketball. Here is a glimpse beneath the apparent formlessness of a professional game, an exploration of individual talents and team objectives which will provide both insight and entertainment into one of the most fascinating of America's sports enterprises. And also one of the most fun.

It's such a simple idea. Take two handy baskets that were once used to transport peaches from farm to market, and hang them above opposite ends of a gymnasium. A balcony overlooks the floor, and it provides a convenient elevation 10 feet high. Gather two sets of players—nine per team originally, because activity was needed to involve a class of eighteen men—and tell them to toss, bounce, stuff, throw, or otherwise propel a large, round ball into the baskets, one per team. At the end of an hour or so of class time, the team that has done this simple thing more often than the rival squad is declared the winner. While you are at it, men, please try to avoid breaking any bones—yours or anyone else's.

This was Dr. James Naismith's original, simple concept in 1891 when he set out to develop a game for his gymnastics class at International Young Men's Christian Association Training School at Springfield, Massachusetts. He sought a game that could be played indoors during winter months under artificial lighting, and which would entertain and encourage good, wholesome physical conditioning in a safe and inexpensive way. The hardy New Englanders weren't averse to crunching physical contact, but the padding used for the flourishing game of football was expensive, and, even in 1891, watching a budget was as much a teacher's responsibility as encouraging learning. Dr. Naismith sought to emphasize quickness and agility and cleverness in his new game and to penalize roughness. At that, he needed thirteen rules to turn his idea into an organized, enjoyable game, and they survive today as the foundations for the enlarged, amended, re-enlarged, and re-amended sets of similar, but differing, rules employed at basketball's several levels of present-day competition—high school, college, amateur, professional, international, women's, and youngsters'.

Running with the basketball under his arm was too easy for a player, especially if his rivals weren't going to be permitted to tackle him, so Dr. Naismith required that the ball be advanced under artificially imposed restrictions. It could be passed from player to player, or a single player could transport it from one side of the court to the other by bouncing it as he moved, a process called *dribbling*. The objective was to get close enough to the basket to permit getting the ball into it as easily as skill and rival defense would allow. If he succeeded in making the basket, the player's team was awarded two points. If he missed, the ball was up for grabs to whoever could retrieve it. Other rules among the original thirteen defined dimensions of the court and time limits, established the concept of the *foul* (physical contact) and the concept of lesser violations (moving the ball out of bounds, failing to dribble, and so forth).

The sport was energetically accepted, following its birth, and soon adopted widely. YMCA teams were organized first, then colleges took up basketball in due time, and even professional teams were started less than ten years after Dr. Naismith's first game.

Just as quickly and enthusiastically, players and coaches discovered flaws in and omissions from the rules, and these had to be brought up to date regularly as the victory-hungry participants and coaches devised ways to exploit them. The original principles of the game remained paramount—to keep a fair balance between offense and defense and to keep mayhem to a minimum. The process of updating rules has never ended, but a third objective is now an even greater concern to some of the rules-writers than the original two: to make the game entertaining for spectators. When a loophole was discovered which permitted teams to employ tactics that were either unfair, dangerous, or dull, it had to be closed. When players' sizes and skills increased to the point that games could become one-sided or boring, rules were changed or added again. Free throws were added to basketball's features early, for instance, to compensate for defensive roughness.

It takes twenty pages of small type in the National Basketball Association Guide to list the league's full set of present rules, but they boil down to the two traditional objectives and the one more recent need, fan interest.

Among basketball's characteristics, and one of the reasons for its continually growing popularity, is that it can be enjoyed even with minimum knowledge of its details. A slamming dunk shot by Wilt Chamberlain, with all the power of his 7-foot-1, 285-pound frame behind it, is as awesomely thrilling to a high-school coed invited to attend her first pro game as it is to the old-timer who's been a fan for years. Anyone who attends games regularly picks up the rules quickly enough. They're readily available in print, too. The thing to grasp isn't the full weight of all the fine print, but what all the regulations are trying to accomplish.

The place to start adding to your fund of knowledge is the playing court itself. Because gymnasiums differ in size, there's latitude in college and high-school ball, but the NBA courts have been standardized for years at 94 feet by 50 feet, divided into 47-foot halves, and marked off in 2-inch lines. The lines begin *outside* the limits of the legal area, remember, and it's just as much a violation to touch an out-of-bounds line as to go fully across it. The baskets of 1891 have long ago been replaced by metal rims 18 inches across, and they're suspended 4 feet inside both ends of the court in the center of backboards 6 feet wide by 4 feet high (constructed of unbreakable glass in most arenas so that they

Wilt Chamberlain—the 16-foot lane only annoys him.

won't obscure end-zone fans' views). The baskets are 10 feet off the floor, and, even for the giants of the NBA, putting a 9-inch-wide basketball through the 18-inch rim at that height is still a challenge.

The free-throw lines are 15 feet from the backboards, bisecting 6-foot circles. The areas from the baselines to the free-throw lines, 16 feet across, are known as the *lanes* and are shaded a different color from the rest of the floor to provide additional emphasis that they're the regions from which field goals can most easily be made. It's obviously desirable for the offensive team to station its biggest, strongest players in that area, and it's obvious, too, what a handicap the defense would be under if it didn't have a way short of mayhem to get the giants out of there. Introduction of the *3-second rule* was an example of the need to keep proper offensive-defensive balance while keeping violence in check. No offensive player may remain in the lane more than 3 seconds without shooting or unless a teammate shoots. The lane used to be just 6 feet across. Topped by the free-throw circle, the area used to look like a keyhole, and the phrase was later shortened to *key*. The width of the lane was fine at 6 feet until basketball saw the emergence of quick, agile giants—the men 7 feet tall, give or take a few inches, who were athletes, not "goons." Even though they were restricted from being in the key for more than 3 seconds, they were still close enough to the basket to score easily—and monotonously. That third dynamic of rules-updating took force, and the lane was widened to 12 feet. When the 7-foot-1 Chamberlain came along to rewrite all the NBA scoring records, the league reacted in the same process by widening the area to its present size.

The dimensions of the court, the locations of the baskets, and the locations and dimensions of the lanes, free-throw circles, and mid-court jump-ball circle have special importance to the players as they struggle back and forth. They offer, too, an additional dimension of entertainment for fans.

Players (at least the outstanding ones) learn to judge exactly where they are on the court and exactly where they are in relation to the baskets by glancing down at the floor and its markings. Fans marvel when an Oscar Robertson or an Earl Monroe sinks a basket seemingly without having looked at the hoop. The shots may be blind, but they're not at all based on luck. Shots *are* taken blindly sometimes, but with confident accuracy because the players know where they

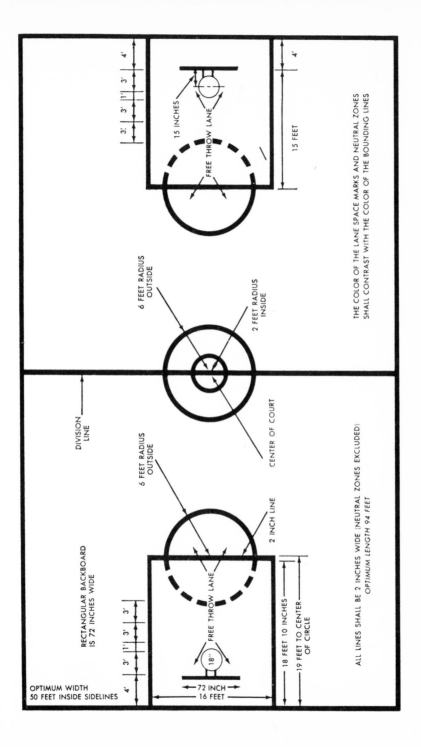

are on the court and, therefore, where they are in relation to the basket. The skill is in getting just enough power behind the shot for accuracy, despite the handicap of facing away from the target. *Blind passes* can be thrown with similar confidence, since the ball-handler can look down to determine where he is, evaluate where a teammate is supposed to be, and pass—blindly—to that spot. It's not a recommended tactic, but it's among the pros' assortments of special tactics for special needs.

Knowledge of the court is valuable to spectators in a different way. If Jerry West or Archie Clark or Sidney Wicks shoots a jumper from the top of the free-throw circle, a quick calculation of the 15 feet from free-throw line to backboard and 3 feet from free-throw line to top of the circle determines that the shot was an 18-footer. Another example: Say time is running out near the end of the third quarter of a game and that Pete Maravich dribbles just inside the midcourt (or *10-second*) stripe, shooting desperately from there just before the buzzer sounds. Whoosh! Two points. Without a tape measure and without surveying equipment, it's easy to know that the shot traveled 43 feet. Halfcourt is 47 feet from either baseline, and the backboard is 4 feet in from the line. Simple subtraction: 43 feet.

In Southern California, sportscaster Chick Hearn has both confounded and entertained fans on his Los Angeles Lakers broadcasts by describing action something like this: "West with the ball, yo-yo dribbles 17 feet out to the right of the key . . . fires . . . hits!" Or he'll describe a field goal as a 22-footer or a 12-footer or whatever. He's not guessing those distances. He's simply keeping in mind the dimensions of the court and, just as do the players, knows the other markings, too. It becomes second nature after a while to use the 15-foot free-throw distance, the 47-foot midcourt line, the 6-foot circles to pinpoint distances and, just as the information adds to Chick's broadcasts, the knowledge can heighten enjoyment from the stands.

That knowing distances and position is so important demonstrates another of basketball's attractions, its rapid motion and its fast pace from one end of the floor to the other. Turnabout and haste are keystones of the game, just as they've been generally in the growth and administration of the sport. Rule changes of even major proportions have been a trademark of basketball, we've seen, even from its infancy. Evolution in the rules and evolution

Pistol Pete Maravich of the Atlanta Hawks launches one of the NBA's sharpest jump shots. (*Courtesy of Martin Blumenthal.*)

in the sizes and skills of players have been traditional too, just as much so as Dr. Naismith's peach baskets. The pattern is constant: If balance between offense and defense is threatened, restore it with a new rule or an amendment to an old one. If roughness begins to get out of hand, change the rules accordingly. If new tactics or a new breed of player threaten to make the game dull, introduce a new concept or update an old one to make basketball exciting again. Players may forget sometimes that sport is a branch of show business, but the owners and general managers never do.

There are sports whose advocates boast that rules have remained unchanged for decades. Happily, basketball (and, in particular, the NBA) has always been dynamic and flexible. To get where it is, it's had to be.

1

STAR OR SUPERSTAR, YOU HAVE TO BE THINKING ALL THE TIME

Oscar Robertson's ball-handling, passing, shooting, rebounding, defensive ability, and cunning have earned him virtually unanimous recognition as the best all-around player in basketball history. At 6-foot-5 and 220 pounds, the Milwaukee Bucks backcourt star is powerful enough to battle on even terms with the game's giants, yet still quick enough to outmaneuver smaller players. "The Big O" has been among the league's leaders in all the major statistical categories every year since he arrived as a professional in 1960 and was an immediate NBA superstar following three All-American seasons at the University of Cincinnati. His talents and his on-court leadership stamp him as the best qualified of all pros to comment on the interplay between thinking and performing physically and on the relationship between the individual and his team.

Oscar Robertson

When I was a boy growing up on the playgrounds and schoolyards of Indianapolis, Indiana, "playing basketball" mostly meant shooting the ball. Shooting was what we learned first and our biggest kick, and most of the time we didn't really play games of basketball, we played "horse." Three or four kids would get together and take turns shooting—the fancier and tougher the shot the better, shots we later learned never to take in a regular game unless we were ready to be really jawboned by our coach. If you made the basket, the next guy was supposed to do it too, from the same place and in the same way you'd shot it. If he missed, he got an *h* and the next guy could try something new. Then the guy after *him* would try to duplicate the shot if it was good. Each time a guy failed to copy another guy's basket successfully, he got another letter and when he got to *h-o-r-s-e* he was out. We kept going until just the winner was left—and then we'd start all over again, until it was too dark or too cold to keep going.

As soon as we graduated to playing more or less regular games, two-on-two or three-on-three and finally five-on-five regular full-court games, we found that we had to have lots of skills besides just shooting, and we also had to learn lots more rules. We went from choose-up-sides playground ball to our first organized teams and from there to high school, college, and, for me, the pros. Each step up you had to be more talented to be able to earn a place on the team, and each step up you had to learn new and more detailed rules.

On the schoolyards, when you goof up it doesn't matter much, except you get mean looks from your teammates. In the pros a mistake can cost you and your team thousands of dollars, so you'd better be sure of what you're doing all the time. No matter how big their stacks of college clippings, rookies are cut early by pro coaches if they don't show brains as well as brawn. I don't care whether you're a sub, a starter, a star, or even a superstar, you've got to be thinking every minute—even if you're on the bench.

The first thing is to know the rules. A lot of them you pick up as you come up from the schoolyards: that you can't dribble with both hands at once; that you can't dribble, hold the ball, then start dribbling again; that teams have to bring the ball across halfcourt within 10 seconds; that a guy can't be in the key more than 3 seconds—the basics. As your coaches work with you and as you study up, the details start coming to you, but no player can ever be *too* familiar with the rules.

Young players sometimes get in trouble because they don't realize certain rules are different in high school and college from the rules in the pros. Take defensive guarding, for example. In high school and college the offensive player has 5 seconds to do something with the ball once he's faced closely by a defender. If he doesn't shoot or pass within the limit when he's hemmed in by the sideline or has stopped his dribble or is trapped in a *double-team* situation (guarded by two men), the referee whistles for a jump ball. There is no such rule in the pros, and I once was able to help win a game for my old team, the Cincinnati Royals, because a rookie who was guarding me hadn't learned the difference. He thought he had me tied up in a corner and was going to get a jump ball. The moment I saw him relax, waiting for the referee's signal, I knew I could get my shot—and I hit it easily because he'd stepped back from guarding me. Imagine how the rook felt when he started to protest and was told to shut up! We won the game by two points, and that rookie had learned a lesson in a painful way. Very painful.

What makes pro ball different from what players get used to in high school and college is the 24-second rule. In the NBA, a team has to attempt a shot within 24 seconds after it gets the ball or lose

Oscar Robertson looks downcourt for passing opportunities, not at the basketball, as he sets up a play for the Milwaukee Bucks despite defensive pressure from Philadelphia's Kevin Loughery.

it out of bounds to the other team. The purpose of the rule is to prevent a team from stalling in the late minutes of a game, protecting a lead. Teams are still permitted to do that in college. It's aggravating to the team that's trailing—and infuriating to fans. Since the 24-second rule was introduced into the NBA in 1954, no pro team has been able just to sit on a lead. You've got to keep going for the hoop, keep putting the ball in the air, and the losing team always has a chance—usually until the last minute or so, anyway—to catch up. Without the 24-second rule, all the losing team can do is try to force a mistake or commit fouls intentionally. For a defensive player just to reach out and wrap his arms around the man with the ball is a big put-down to fans who pay to see action, but at least there'll be some free throws to be shot, and at least the trailing team can take over the ball out of bounds after the score. *With* the clock, though, the team that's behind knows it will have a chance at the ball one way or another, and there's not the same urgent need to foul.

What the members of the NBA Board of Governors were hopeful of doing by introducing the 24-second rule was to keep games exciting and stop the excessive intentional fouling that was so boring and—when the fouling got overly rough—more and more often resulting in fights and injuries. Actually, the governors accomplished much more than just speeding up the game. The 24-second rule changed basketball so much that the pro game and the college version are now almost two different sports. Pro ball is the player's game, college ball more a battle between two coaches.

In college and high-school ball, with plenty of time to work for the best possible percentage shot, teams can use complicated offenses with maybe three or four passes planned before the ball gets to the man who's supposed to take the shot. Defenses are under pressure for as much as a minute at a time to try to break up plays. In pro ball, everything speeds up tremendously. There's no time to try to work complicated plays. You use up some of your 24 seconds getting the ball into your half of the court, and you can make one pass, maybe two. Then you'd better get the ball in the air, because, if you don't, that buzzer's going to sound off in a hurry. Most of the time, actually, pro teams don't even use planned plays at all. Instead, they try to *fast break* whenever they can, trying for the quickest and best shot possible. The little passes and handoffs and *picks* one man sets for another to block off or screen off a defensive player are part of what we call *free-lancing*. The defense is able to concentrate on stopping the other team for just a short period, which means it can use much different—but not necessarily easier to perform—strategy from college teams. The one advantage college teams have is that they can use what are called *zone defenses,* each man playing an area of the floor rather than guarding a specific offensive player. The NBA banned the zone defense when it introduced the 24-second rule, because the players back then hadn't developed the quick jump shot and had trouble scoring against zones. Today's pros can fire the ball much more quickly and from more places on the court than the players who were in the league in the early days—but that's because the 24-second clock forced development of new tactics and put the premium on quickness. Big, ponderous guys who couldn't race up and down the court, switching in an instant from offense to defense and back again, couldn't tolerate the new tempo. They became as extinct in the NBA as dinosaurs, and their places were taken by the new breed of player— fast, quick-handed and quick-witted, and nowadays just as big!

In the new tempo games are won or lost in an instant. Not only do you have to keep running up and down the floor, keep changing your thinking from offense to defense, you've also got to keep in mind every possible factor. How much time is left in the quarter? How much time is left on the 24-second clock? How many fouls on your team? How many on the other team? How many fouls on you and how many on the guy guarding you? What's the score? How many time outs do you have left? It's incredible all the things you have to consider. The coach yells out reminders and instructions all the time, but in the split second when you've got to decide whether or not to shoot, whether or not to gamble defensively or play it safe, you're on your own. You can't wait for advice from the bench.

Another aspect of relating to your team is what each player's contribution ought to be toward winning. Ego is something you have to take into account. Every athlete enjoys glory. It's great to hear the fans cheering for you when you make a spectacular play. It's great to read a story about how you starred in a game. Glory is one reason you work as hard as you do. Every player is guilty of going on an ego trip now and then, and that's all right—as long as he's not hurting his team. Teamwork is fundamental at every level of basketball. That means passing up a shot if another player is open for a better one. That means helping out on defense. That means being more interested in the final score than in the individual statistics. Where the NBA game is different from school ball in defining teamwork is that it also means being willing to become a specialist. If every player were equally skillful at every phase of basketball, there wouldn't be that problem. The truth is that some players are bigger and stronger than others, some are better shooters than others, some are better ball-handlers, and some are better rebounders. I don't mean that some players are absolutely helpless trying to do one thing or another—you can't make the pros if you have a basic weakness. But every player who's played enough ball to graduate up to the pros develops his favorite moves, his favorite shots, his best set of skills—his *style,* in other words.

What has developed in pro basketball over the years is a basic pattern for putting together a five-man starting unit. Coaches work, in a way, just like an expert chef. They try to combine different ingredients into a successful recipe. Coaches, generally speaking, try for one forward on their teams who's a point-getter—a guy like John Havlicek, Bob Love, Cazzie Russell, Sidney Wicks, or Connie Hawkins—a guy who can shoot and do a decent job of rebounding. At the other forward, they look for a bigger type of guy, an especially tough rebounder and defensive player, a sacrificing kind of player like Paul Silas or Dave DeBusschere or Bill Bridges. The model centers are Kareem Abdul-Jabbar, Wilt Chamberlain, Elmore Smith, Nate Thurmond—big, active guys who can score from underneath, dominate the rebounding, block shots, generally take charge. The ideal balance for guards is kind of like the pattern for cornermen. One guard's job, in this ideal line-up we're describing, is to be able to score from outside, or by driving and being a playmaker, too. I'm that kind of player, and so are Dave Bing, Jerry West, Archie Clark, and Pete Maravich, for example. The second guard's job is defense, helping handle the ball, things which mesh with what the "No. 1 guard" does best. Most coaches look for some size at that position, and also for a player who keeps moving so that if the shooting guard is double-teamed defensively, he can pass to his partner in the open for an easy shot. Players like that are Gail Goodrich, Kevin Loughery, Dickie Garrett, Jon McGlocklin. Analyze the starting line-ups for most teams, and you'll find more or less what I'm talking about. If teams could just sign any player they wanted to, they probably would set up something like this type of balance of five men. Since teams have to build through the draft system, though, it's much harder to get that perfect blend. Coaches go crazy trying to reach it with the personnel available to them, figuring ways to make up for what their squads lack.

The lesson in all this for the young player is to be patient before starting to develop an individual style. A young player really ought to be patient even before concentrating on learning a single position on the floor. At age twelve or thirteen it's hard to judge how tall a boy eventually is going to be, and there's not much sense in concentrating on learning to play center if later he's going to have to try to make a team by being a guard. It doesn't make much sense, either, to concentrate just on shooting, for instance, because, no matter how good a shot you may be, you might wind up on the same team with a man trying for the same position you're trying to earn, yet even a *better* shooter. Instead, boys ought to try to develop all their skills while they're young, then start to specialize as they see what their final physical make-up will be. Style develops naturally as a combination of skill, personality, quickness (or lack of it), and size.

Let me give another couple of examples. Both Jerry West, when he played at West Virginia University, and I, at the University of Cincinnati, were forwards in college. Jerry was big enough to play the front line at 6-foot-3, and I was 6-foot-5—about the same size as most of the guys we had to guard and who were guarding us. When we became pros after playing together on the United States Olympic team in 1960, we both had to switch and become guards. There must be thirty or forty guys every year trying out for pro teams, guys about 6-5 or 6-4, who were forwards in college but haven't developed their dribbling and other skills enough to learn to play guard. They get cut. In the pros, you've got to produce *now!* Coaches can't afford to be patient.

Let me show another example of why it's important to try to become a versatile player. Howie Komives, who plays with Buffalo now, was originally drafted by the New York Knicks. As a college senior at Bowling Green University in Ohio, he averaged more than 32 points a game and led the whole country in scoring. Shooting was his game, and shooting was how he figured he'd make his mark as a pro. When he got to the Knicks, he found himself trying for the vacant job as the partner in the backcourt for Dick Barnett, who was just one of the most fantastic shooters in history, that's all. Luckily for Howie, the Knicks' guard situation at that time—before they became one of the best teams in the league—was pretty thin. He had made himself a good ball-handler and good playmaker even though he was a much, much better shooter, and he earned himself a job—not the job he'd planned, but a starting spot on an NBA team. The Knicks got all the shooting they needed from Barnett, so Komives assumed other responsibilities and has been a top pro ever since.

The thing is, a team's situation changes from year to year as older players retire and new ones come along. Every player has to adjust. Some seasons, I've been on teams with lots of scoring ability at all positions. Those seasons, I've been able to play loose and cool, to score or pass or concentrate on defense—whatever the game situation seemed to require. Other seasons, I've been on teams with a shortage of offensive threats, and those years I had to concentrate on putting points on the scoreboard, even at the risk (because you only have so much energy to burn, after all) of slacking off a little on other parts of my game. Wilt Chamberlain is a player who's adjusted from season to season, too. Early in his career, he played with teams that needed his 40 or 50 points a night to have a decent chance to win. When he played with different teams later on, teams that had more players who could score consistently, he concentrated on rebounding, passing, and defense.

Basketball demands teamwork, whichever way a team plays, but teamwork can mean lots of things, depending on the situation. We're in business as pros, and the business is winning. You have a job to do and you do it—or somebody comes along to do it for you and you start thinking about some other line of work.

2

OFFENSE OR DEFENSE, A WIN IS A WIN

The final buzzer sounds and the scoreboard shows one team with 135 points, the other with 125. Another night, another place, with two other teams having played, the final score is 110–100. In either case, one club has logged an entry in its "win" column, and another has lost. Is there anything to choose between the two situations? Plenty, according to two major schools of basketball thinkers —those who favor offense and those who favor defense.

For one group the objective is to roll up as great a points total as possible, overwhelming the foe with sheer force of scoring momentum. To the other group, the choice of tactics offering best assurance of victory most often is to devote greater attention in planning and in practice sessions to limiting the opposition's scoring, recording its own points as a matter of course.

Perhaps that's stating the contrast a bit too strongly. Basketball is unique, among many things, for its constant flow from one side of the court to the other, from offense to defense. Even within this framework, however, there are some teams that are more strongly oriented toward scoring, others which are basically defensive in their approach.

Individual players tend toward one concept or the other too, because of their early coaching and because of their personal styles of play and physical make-up. Billy Cunningham, the leaping star of the Philadelphia 76ers until a court-imposed move to the ABA in 1972, is offense personified, even though he is an accomplished defender. A former All-American, the 6-foot-7, 215-pound all-star forward is a blitzkrieg scorer on drives to the basket as well as with his accurate outside jump shots. Walt Frazier of the New York Knicks, on the other hand, is regarded as perhaps the NBA's finest defensive player, big and strong as well as quick at 6-foot-4, 205 pounds. A high-scoring forward as a collegian at Southern Illinois University, Frazier has made a smooth transition to his present role as a leading backcourt performer.

Winning is a habit for both players, but they have different outlooks on how to turn that habit from an objective into a reality.

Billy Cunningham

People who meet me for the first time, people who know from the press books that I went to college at the University of North Carolina, get a puzzled look on their faces when they hear me speak. I may have gone to a Dixie university, but it doesn't take people long to figure, when they listen to me, that before I ever saw Chapel Hill I was brought up in Brooklyn, New York, U.S.A. I'm a city kid, and my first basketball was scuffling around the schoolyards—like a lot of my fellow pros. I played at Erasmus Hall High School in Flatbush, was lucky to do well there and was fortunate to be offered several scholarships for college. I selected UNC.

The point is that my basketball thinking was shaped in my boyhood, when the guy who got the most respect was the guy who was the best shooter, the guy who scored the most points. I'm more sophisticated in my basketball outlook now, and I know that great defense is a feature of any championship team, but that early training I got in the quick-moving, high-scoring Eastern style of ball stays with me. I work hard at my defensive assignments, but I know that my vital responsibility is to get my team points. I happen to think that playing the game with scoring as your biggest objective is the best way to play, and for me the most enjoyable.

Offense means taking the initiative. When you've got the ball, *you* decide whether to go left, go right, take the shot, pass, whatever. It's up to the defense to react, and no matter how quick the defense may be, it's still going to be a split second behind. The team with the ball calls the shots, in other words. If it's your team that forces the tempo and style of the game, if it's your team that's taking charge, the other team has got to work at trying to stop you, and usually that means it has to sacrifice *its* offensive thinking. In other words, I believe in going full speed right from the start, moving the ball and moving myself, forcing the team I'm playing to worry about stopping me and therefore to neglect its own scoring.

Another thing that shapes my thinking is that offense seems more natural to me. My first memories of basketball are shooting the ball, not trying to keep somebody else from shooting. Give a youngster a ball and show him a hoop, even if he's never seen a basketball game in his life, and he'll try to shoot. I don't know why shooting seems so natural, I just know that it is. And I also know that playing defense isn't natural at all—it's hard work, if you're doing it correctly. You never seem to tire when you're trying to score, but your legs can feel like spaghetti and your lungs can feel like they're on fire when the other team has the ball and you're trying to shut them off.

Another thing about offense: It's what fans like to see. People get excited about the guys who make fantastic shots a lot easier than they do about guys who stop those shots, and, because it's the people who buy tickets who pay my salary, I'm all too aware that basketball is part of show business.

I'm a product of Eastern ball, remember, which means a lot of passing, a lot of movement, working to get myself or one of my teammates loose for an easy shot. In Eastern ball, you follow certain basic ideas offensively in order to get that easy shot, rather than using complicated plays the way teams in other parts of the country do. For instance, a basic rule of basketball is to keep the ball moving, to try to pass the ball as quickly as you can, and then to run to some open place on the floor—*pass and cut,* it's called. By doing this, you keep the defense moving, too. When the defense moves too late or moves in one direction while the ball goes to somebody in the other direction, your team gets that easy shot. This idea of play is so basic it's what guys do when they get together on pickup teams or when a bunch of pros get together for all-star games. They work smoothly together even if they've never played together before as a five-man unit.

Even more basic in basketball is the running game, the fast break. The idea is to gèt the ball downcourt in a hurry, before the defense can get settled down and in assigned positions. The most usual, basic situation is the man with the ball facing a man trying to stop him from shooting—*one-on-one,* in technical terms. You fake one way, fake another, fake a jump or fake a drive, move your hip, move your head, do anything to get the defensive man going the wrong way and—*zap!* Two points. That's my game, that's Jerry West's game, that's Earl Monroe's game, that's the way lots of pros work best. It takes *moves* to play that way, and you've got to be able to shoot quickly, before the defensive player has. time to recover.

Teams that don't have players who are good at one-on-one ball use other tactics. One use of free-lancing is to have one player stand stationary to *screen* or *pick* the defensive player, so that the man with the ball can get off a good shot. The man with the ball can dribble behind a stationary teammate to get room between himself and a defensive player, or a player without the ball goes to a spot he sees the defender will run into if he keeps up with the dribbler, which is the difference between a screen and a pick. These situations are what teams are trying to earn when they use what we call *set plays* or *set patterns* offensively, creating screen and pick situations on a planned rather than improvised basis. It takes practice to perfect plays or to get guys naturally setting screens and picks, and timing is a vital thing. The screen or pick and the shot have to come at almost the same time, or the defense can readjust. The difference between plays and patterns is simple. Plays mean definite routes that guys run, with or without the ball, leading to a situation at which a definite player takes a definite, preplanned shot. In pattern offenses there's no definite moment for the shot to be taken, but with all five offensive players in motion there's going to be a mistake made by a defender, someone is going to get open, and if he gets the ball in time he'll have a shot. One of the things an offense tries to earn with either plays or patterns is a crisscross which forces defensive players to *switch* from guarding their assigned man onto another, hopefully with a size or quickness advantage in your favor—a 6-foot guard trying to defend against the offensive team's 6-foot-7 forward, for example, or what's called a *mismatch.*

Taller players, of course, have the natural advantage because a taller man can get off a good shot over the man guarding him, even though that defensive man may have played exactly by the book and even though he has avoided being faked out of position. An ideal situation for your team is to force the defense to change its basic line-up, even putting in a big man to try to guard your big man or a quick man to guard your quick man. Even if the change succeeds in stopping your player from scoring easy baskets, you've still got an overall advantage because you're going with your best five players and still have the initiative, while the other team has had to give up its regular line-up.

Mel Counts is a tremendously valuable player, to name one guy often involved in mismatches, because he's a 7-footer but still a good enough outside shooter and quick enough to play forward (7-footers otherwise are pretty much obliged to play center). John Havlicek is another player who gives opponents fits because he's so quick, but plays forward at 6-foot-5 (and also lots of guard). At one time they both played for the Boston Celtics, back when Red Auerbach was coaching. The Celtics were an enormous headache for my team and every other team in the NBA in those days—just as they still are, for different reasons. Counts would come into a game for them and have a 5- or 6-inch advantage over the man playing against him. Mel would get three or four quick baskets with outside shots over his man's head with that big reach of his, and we'd have to send in a big man at forward to stop him. Auerbach would then call Havlicek in to replace Counts, and then *he'*d get three or four quick baskets against the big, usually slower, big man who'd been guarding Counts. We'd make another substitution to settle things down again, but by that time the Celtics had maybe a 10-point lead and we'd be so dizzy from trying to balance things defensively that we had a horrible time getting organized offensively ourselves.

I don't mean to put down defense. It's just that, in my thinking, an offensive outlook is the best way to play, the most fun way to play, and the best way to have the best chance of winning most games. An offensive outlook also doesn't necessarily mean you play relaxed defense, which the Lakers proved in the 1971–72 season by recording that amazing 33-game winning streak of theirs and then winning the playoffs. They played tremendous defense that season, but, even at that, the Lakers were a team oriented offensively. If

I hadn't been so busy trying to figure a way to beat them, I'd probably have been on the sidelines cheering like crazy, because they certainly were my kind of team.

Coaches and players of Cunningham's viewpoint are those content at those 135–125 victories, or 154–132, like a game the Lakers won over Philadelphia during their streak. Walt Frazier represents those who feel 110–100 games can be every bit as exciting as the adding-machine-score games, and more consistently within an average team's reach. The 6-foot-4 all-NBA defensive all-star from Southern Illinois U proved his point, among other instances, when he scored the Knicks' last 13 points in a 101–99 upset win over Milwaukee in January of 1972, in a game in New York that opened the national television schedule.

Walt Frazier

Anyone who thinks defense is dull has never been at Madison Square Garden in the final minutes of an NBA game when my team, the Knicks, has a victory pretty well locked up, with the team we're playing still under 100 points. Our fans—the most aware rooters anywhere, because basketball is New York's game—cheer up a storm every time a shot by the other team misses, moan when a shot goes through the hoop. They take even more pride in our keeping an opponent from reaching the century mark than the players, I think, and the pride gives us a big lift. The year we won the world championship for the first time, the fans' enthusiastic rooting was a big pickup for us, in fact, because our players seemed to get extra quickness, extra power to jump high, extra willingness to work hard from the excitement of it all.

To me, the biggest thing about defense is that it's something you can rely on. Sure, it's more fun to score baskets than to stop them, but it's also possible to be more consistent stopping the other team than worrying mostly about your own score. Shooting is a knack, a talent. Shooting accurately means having your rhythm right, feeling good, being cool. It's great to have those nights, not just because you get the loudest cheers or because your name is going to be in the next day's headlines, but just because it feels so good right then, the moment you let go a shot. You know immediately, before the ball's halfway to the hoop, that it's going to be pure string music—right through the net without even kissing the rim. The problem is that you never know when you're going to go salty. You never know when you're going to have a night you can hardly hit the backboard, much less hit the basket. Offense is inconsistent because it's touch and feel and talent. Defense, because it mostly means being willing to work hard, is something to rely on night after night, game after game.

The other thing about defense is that it seems to open up every other part of basketball for you. There are lots of nights over the course of the long NBA season—we start in September and we're still playing in March and, if we make the playoffs, even April and May—when you're exhausted from travel and from playing four or five nights in a row. You start the game and you just drag. But you gut it out, play your "D," and pretty soon you start to get with it. Maybe I make a steal or maybe Willis Reed blocks a shot, we get a cheap basket or two, and suddenly we're rolling. You forget how tired you are, and pretty soon basketball is beautiful again. The shot you missed by 3 feet five minutes ago all of a sudden is the easiest thing in the world.

That's the way the Knicks play, anyway, and we started to become a great team when we all realized what our coach, Red Holzman, was trying to get us to accomplish—even though everybody on the team was more famous for scoring than for defense. We work as a team on defense, gambling for the steal at times, but knowing that another player will help cover for us if the gamble doesn't work. We play a forcing type of defense, which we feel takes away some of the offense's advantage of initiative, and we try to keep the other team so worried about not making mistakes and not being embarrassed that we take away its concentration and its rhythm. When things go right for us, we control the game and we get lots of easy shots. We win. That's the important thing.

The Knicks' type of defense is something new in pro ball, a style other teams have copied in the last couple of years. It's a combination of the two basic types of defense that are played in high-school and college ball—man-to-man and zone. In the first type of defense you start out assigned to a specific player on the other team and you follow him all over the court, trying to keep him from getting the

The cat-quick reflexes that help Walt Frazier escape from Golden State Warrior Ron Williams become even more valuable to the New York Knicks star when he plays defense.

ball altogether and, if he does get it, trying to keep him from scoring. Playing man-to-man defense, you've also got to be ready to *switch*, or let your man go while you tail a new offensive player because there's been a crisscross maneuver that screens you from your original man. The offensive team is trying to *force* that switch, trying to get the shot because the switch either hasn't been made or because it's been made too late or too sloppily to work. In zone defense, which isn't allowed in the NBA any more, you don't guard a specific man, you guard an area of the court, responsible for shutting off any shots from your zone. Switches aren't necessary when you're playing this kind of defense, and this tends to cut down the offense's opportunity to drive for baskets. Instead, teams playing against zone defenses try to concentrate on passing, trying to catch you in the wrong part of your zone and opening up outside shooting opportunities. It's a game in which the ball moves while the players tend to be more stationary, at least in theory, and zone defenses tend to be more passive. You *react* in zone defense more than *force,* which is probably the reason college and high-school coaches generally favor man-to-man. Quick players seem to play better that way, but coaches who have bigger, slower teams with a tendency to commit a lot of fouls usually prefer to play zone. It's obvious why the NBA outlawed the zone when it introduced the 24-second rule —there's more action guaranteed that way.

The Knicks, Buffalo, and several other teams play a defense that tries to combine the best features of both those styles—we play man-to-man, with some zone principles. We start out assigned to a man, but we also concentrate on where the ball is, trying to force the offense to spread out and to keep the ball away from the basket. We'll try to get a man trapped against an out-of-bounds line, and then a second Knick will leave his assigned man to create a two-against-one, or double-team situation. There are many great dribblers in the NBA and lots of outstanding passers, but with two against one the odds are in our favor. Sure, there'll be one offensive player left open. We want that. We're daring the man with the ball to try to throw it to the open man. Usually that unguarded player is some place way across the floor, though, and when the ball-handler tries to pass such a long distance one of us is probably going to be down the court. Zap an offense a few times in a row for easy breakaway baskets that way, and pretty soon they get too cautious, hold on to the ball for fear they'll make a mistake, even though a man may get wide open. Maybe just the opposite will happen, particularly with a young player or a young team—our pressure tactics will destroy their poise altogether, rattle them into even *more* errors. Either way, we get the advantage. We wind up getting not only easier baskets but also more of them.

Playing at the Garden, the Knicks have that special edge we get from our fans. When Dave DeBusschere or Bill Bradley or I force a steal and drive for a basket, the place goes crazy. The team that's been burned feels all that much more embarrassed, and we seem to get a boost of adenalin, a new burst of energy. It's a beautiful feeling. You're twelve feet tall, you can't do anything wrong, and all the screaming and cheering is music to your ears. Defense dull? Maybe some places, but definitely not in the Garden. We'll settle for our 110 points any night—as long as the other team doesn't have more than 109. And only 99 is even a greater groove than that!

3

THE SWEETEST SOUND
ON EARTH: SWISH!

Every man is ten years old again when he stands below a 10-foot-high metal hoop with a basketball in his hands. Be he veteran professional player reporting to a cold and silent arena for an off-day practice session, or a paunchy businessman pausing on a neighborhood playground to chauffeur home his youngster in time for dinner, there is a fascination there that is seductive. "Try me . . . try me . . . try me," the ball calls, promising fundamental, emotional, sensual gratification if only it's tossed accurately enough. Every man knows this exhilarating sensation who has ever heard the sweet swish of a basketball descending cleanly through a net—or heard the delicate little "plop" of a crumpled piece of office stationery landing in a wastebasket.

In either case, certain elements of hand-and-eye coordination are the same. But an office worker's impishly irrelevant imitation of Jerry West and West's actual demonstration of his "Mr. Clutch" accuracy with hundreds of thousands of dollars at stake in an NBA playoff game are hardly the same thing. The office worker's day dream imagines the glory of being recognized as the most picture-perfect, most consistently accurate jump shooter of all time. West's demonstration of that skill in a playoff game is the result of years of work spent perfecting it.

Jerry West

Bill Sharman, who was a great star for the Boston Celtics while I was still a youngster, was kind to pay me a big compliment during our first year of working together as coach and player for the Los Angeles Lakers. "Jerry West is not just a superstar," he told reporters during our fantastic 33-game winning streak in 1972, "he is a superstar at both ends of the court." That meant something, coming from Bill, not only because he's an outstanding coach, but also because he was such a great player at my position himself. What pleased me more than just being praised by my coach— even stars enjoy being on the good side of their coaches—was that I've always taken pride at working hard on defense as well as on being an offensive star. That's what "playing at both ends" means— offensive work at one side of the floor, defense at the other.

At the same time it would be shortsighted of me not to recognize that my most important responsibility on the Lakers—for most of my career—has been to put the ball in the basket. I may be embarrassed to have had the "Mr. Clutch" nickname hung on me, but at least I recognize that the "clutch" part refers to making baskets, not to my clutching somebody on the other team to keep him from scoring. I've enjoyed the thrill of being able to win games for the Lakers by hitting shots with time running out, but I've had the agony of failure too. Once, I shot a miserable 6-for-27 in a world-championship game against the Boston Celtics—in 1965, I recall it was—shots I usually hit fairly easily. I had to keep putting the ball up even though I was having such a bad night. That was my job. If you're a shooter, you keep trying, adjusting if you can, because you hope that suddenly you'll figure out what you're doing wrong. The Lakers lost that game—and eventually the title series— and I don't remember anybody calling me Mr. Clutch that night, by the way.

The way I look at basketball, shooting is a matter of three big, over-all considerations. First, you've got to know when to shoot and from where to shoot. You need a "theory" of shooting, in other words. Second, you have to know how to get room and time for your shot, as well as what type of shot to attempt. Finally, no matter what shot you decide you ought to try, you've got to use correct mechanical technique or all you'll do is give somebody a chance to get a rebound. Some players may disagree with my thinking about shooting, may emphasize some part of thinking or mechanics over another, but I think my ideas are shared by the majority of NBA players and coaches.

My idea is that a player should always try for the surest shot possible—or closest, which may be the same thing. But a player also should be careful not to pass up shots out of self-doubt. No one can be a 60-per-cent shooter all over the court, but you develop spots where you're 75- or 80-per-cent, an NBA must. Most nights my jump shot is accurate out to about 22 feet or so, but I'm more accurate from 15 to 18, and I'd rather shoot dunkers like Wilt Chamberlain—if I could, that is. If I'm open, naturally I'll take my shot. First, I check three things: (1) that I'm within what I have learned is my good percentage range, (2) that I've got time to set up for my shot with good balance, and (3) that no one else on my team is open for a better shot than I am (and in a position to which I can pass safely to him). Even if I were not as accurate a shooter as I've gotten the reputation for being, I'd still be sure to take my shot if I were open. This is because it's so vital to an offensive team to have every man be a legitimate scoring threat who must be "played honest."

Gail Goodrich, my backcourt partner with the Lakers, is a good example of how a player helps his team by taking his good shots when he has the chance. Being "unselfish" and passing up scoring chances isn't a virtue at all, despite what fans may think. Because Gail is an outstanding shooter and dangerous from any place on the court, defenses must assign a man to guard him. When they put a man on Gail, that means they can't have two men guarding me. I've got my one man, and Gail has his defender, and we both get our share of good, open shots. Early in the 1971–72 season, before teams realized how much Gail had improved himself over the previous summer by working hard on some special drills to improve his quickness and stamina, they were double-teaming me a lot. That left Gail open a lot of times, and often I was able to pass to him for easy shots. Fortunately for all of us, Gail wasn't bashful about putting the ball up, and he helped me win the 1971–72 assists championship that way. If he'd gotten self-conscious about shooting as often as he did some nights, or if he hadn't hit such a high percentage of his shots, it would have been perfect for the other teams' strategies. The big lesson for all players is this: Work on your shooting so you're as dangerous as possible (with special, super-accuracy areas), take your shot when you're open—but be sure the shot you take is a good one for you. Whether it's a good shot to take depends on a player's range, accuracy, and available time to get good balance and position.

Getting open for easy shots—off the fast break or in play situations—depends partly on individual ability and individual style, partly on the position you play on the team. As a guard, I find that most of my shots develop as I move toward the basket. A forward shoots more from the corners or up close. And a center shoots most of his shots starting with his back actually to the basket.

In my game, I usually earn my shooting opportunities by working with fakes and by my quickness against the man guarding me. Another way some players get their opportunities is to keep moving, looking for open spaces and being ready to take a pass from the man with the ball. I work more with the ball than without it, and my style is to fake one thing, then do another—do anything that will give me that bit of time I need to shoot. I may pretend I'm going to drive toward the basket for a layup, then, instead, stop short and jump-shoot; I wait for that moment I have my man back on his heels, ready to try to stop my faked drive. Another time I may fake going up for a jump but, instead of leaving my feet, I wait for my man to go up on his toes or actually to jump up. When

Joe Ellis of the Golden State Warriors forces Jerry West to drive to his left—
but Jerry will still get his shot.

he goes for my faked jump, I can scoot around him for a layup.

This man-against-man situation is one of the absolutely fundamental parts of basketball, going one-on-one. A player who is good at both the outside shot and the drive gives a defensive player nothing but agony, and all pro players, no matter what position they play, try to develop their outside-inside ability. A player who isn't quick enough or cute enough to work well one-on-one can still be a successful pro if he is an outstanding outside shooter whose talents help a team in other ways. Jeff Mullins of the Golden State Warriors is a key man for his team because his outside shot is good. Jeff doesn't have quite the quickness to be a great one-on-one man, but the Warriors work lots of plays setting up screens and picks for him. When he gets shooting room, he's as tough as anybody in the league.

A common thing among good shooters is that they all are fairly quick taking their shots once they decide they're open. Through the years, shooting has evolved in this direction. Early, the shot most players used was the two-handed set shot. It was accurate from far outside, but took time to set up for and launch. Hank Luisetti, the great Stanford University star of just before World War II, helped modernize things by setting all sorts of records with his one-hand shot. The big explosion in scoring came when players took Luisetti's shot a step farther and turned it into the jump shot, a maneuver that requires practically no time at all between decision to shoot and the shot itself.

Good balance is necessary to shoot the jumper or any other shot. No shot is a good percentage shot, no matter how close to the hoop, if it's taken from an awkward position. The ball should be held with the fingertips of the shooting hand, just far enough back in the hand to be felt lightly with the palm. You cradle it in the V formed by the thumb and index finger. The elbow must be kept fairly close to the body and directly under the hand through the entire shot. The left hand (if you're a right-handed shooter) supports and guides the ball, and the lift comes from the legs in a smooth sweep followed by a downward, slightly inward snap of the wrist and a good extension of hand and arm in which the index finger acts sort of as the aiming device. The arch of the shot depends on personal preference, but you have to be able to adjust to get it over the defense—a big arch if you're trying to keep it from being blocked by Wilt Chamberlain, less of an arch for smaller defense men. For a backcourt player, the best target seems to me to be the back part of the rim, about in the center. Coach Sharman preaches to us that the ball is about 9 inches across and the hoop is about 18. If you shoot for the middle, you've got the best possible margin for error to either side. If your shot is too long, it still may hit the backboard and get the benefit of the bounce back down and through the basket. If the shot is short, a good follow-through will put backspin on the ball and it may go up in the air softly off the iron and possibly drop through. I try to keep my eye on my target through the entire shooting process and to see where the ball hits. By doing that, I can adjust for a miss—go a little more to one side or the other, shoot harder or softer, according to where I miss. Another little trick is to shoot a little harder as the game goes on, to compensate for loss of power as fatigue begins to catch up with you.

Notice that I haven't said anything about the height of the jump on this shot. I've found that height doesn't matter that much, but that quickness and good balance are vital. I suggest that players just take a natural jump, concentrating on going straight up and releasing the shot just about at the top of the jump in one smooth, continuous motion. In practice, I pick spots on the court, move to them, jump, shoot, and try to come down in exactly the same spot as my last footsteps. Besides making my shot more accurate, coming down that way and in good balance gives me the chance either to go after my rebound, hustle back to the other end of the court for defense, or to start moving into a new play if we get the rebound. A player like Earl Monroe or Bob Love will use a number of fakes to get open for their shot, but, for me, sometimes the best fake is no fake at all. I rely on my quickness in getting away my shot, even though the man playing me may be playing me very tight.

Close guarding is something any shooter learns to expect. You don't mind it unless the referees let things get out of hand. I've had men grab my hips so hard and try to keep me from going where I want to (this is what's called *hand-checking*) that afterward you can almost see their fingerprints on my skin. Other guys wait until you're up in the air and vulnerable, then poke you or nudge you off-balance. It's very frustrating when this happens, and it's one reason I was personally so grateful that the Lakers have emphasized the fast break the last couple of seasons. I'm called "Mr. Clutch," you might say, but more often I feel like "Mr. Clutched"!

The quickness of Jerry West helps make his jump shot one of the most devastating weapons in NBA history. His mongoose-swift moves help him, too, to perform those things noted by Bill Sharman in calling the great Laker a "superstar at both ends of the court." Indiana U grad Jon McGlocklin of the Milwaukee Bucks doesn't have West's speed, but he has perfected his own shooting style and game to the point where he's one of the NBA's more effective performers too.

Jon McGlocklin

Every time I put on my uniform and tie my sneakers before a game, I say a special little silent thanks to the good luck I've had in my pro basketball career. It took a while, but I play with teammates best suited to my style. I could be selling insurance back in Indiana, otherwise.

I've got good size—6-foot-5, about 205 pounds—but I'm not big or strong enough to be successful full-time as a forward, my position in college. It's been a problem for me because, you might say, I make up for my lack of size by also being slow. Oh, I might whip the average person in a footrace, but being slightly better than average speed isn't enough in the NBA; there are too many players with superspeed. Realizing I'd never dazzle too many people with my footwork, but ambitious to make it in the NBA, I've learned to make myself valuable to my team by working hard on defense and by developing my outside shot.

Originally I was drafted by the Cincinnati Royals. I played at least a little bit in most games for the Royals for two seasons, but never became a regular because, among other things, the Royals were a small team that had to rely as much as possible on speed. In 1967 I became a member of a brand-new club, the San Diego

Rockets. That was a club without much size too, and I didn't get as much playing time as I'd have liked, although I couldn't honestly second-guess my coach for the way he was using me. Another new franchise was organized the next season, the Milwaukee Bucks, and I was selected by the new club in the expansion draft. I got to play quite a bit more with this team, my third, and I gained self-confidence. Our second season a rookie joined us. He not only made us an instant contender, but also helped me become more valuable to my team than I'd ever been before.

The new player was Lew Alcindor (in 1971 he asked that we call him by another name, Kareem Abdul-Jabbar, which he'd adopted when he joined the Islamic religion) and he created problems for opposing teams that were so great every other player on our team—including me—was able to benefit. Where my game had been an all-around kind of responsibility before, I could concentrate more on outside shooting after Kareem came along. Zeroing in on the hoop from farther out and being able to hit fairly consistently, I helped not only myself but also Kareem and every other frontcourt player on the team too.

Kareem is so great a close-in threat, you see, that teams who play us tend to try to *collapse* on him. That is, they try to keep him under some control by having their center play him tight from behind, pushing a lot, having their forwards sort of pinch in from the sides, and having their guards retreat back to where he's just about surrounded. I stay outside, with plenty of room usually between me and my "collapsing" defensive man. With that great reach and team-play outlook of Kareem's, he's looking for some player on our team to be open when he has the ball. If I'm the man to whom he passes, I've got a fair chance of scoring by actually starting my shot even before his pass gets to me. I sort of aim for the back rim and start my move as I catch the ball. I move my feet to shooting stance, dip my knees, and line up my elbow in just about the same motion as catching the ball, and I dip my knees according to how much power I need to reach the hoop. My shooting motion is the same as a jump shot, except that I just barely get off my feet. Shooting from as far outside as I do, with Kareem and our forwards under the hoop, I don't worry so much about following up my shot for a possible rebound as a Jerry West, for instance, but I do make sure that I finish with a good follow-through and good balance. My job is to get back quickly on defense once I've taken my shot. When I play guard, that is. When I play forward, now and then, I have to keep rebounding more in mind.

My outside shooting gives teams we play second thoughts. They have to decide whether shutting Kareem off inside by collapsing or *sagging* on him is worth permitting me and our other players to snipe away from outside. If they extend their defense to protect against the outside shot, then we try to set up Kareem by passing to him when he wants the ball—which is after he gets to the position on the floor he's trying to establish.

There's another option open to me too, and that's to fool people with the quickness I do have. I'm not supposed to be quick enough to be a good driver, so now and then, when my defensive man comes up tight on me to guard against my set shot, I scoot around him and try for the layup. The shock of my trying to drive sometimes gives me lots of room and lots of time. The razzing I get from our fans and from my teammates reminds me not to get delusions of speed just because I've fooled somebody once. I don't try this play very often.

When Oscar Robertson joined the Bucks in 1970, my job became even a little bit easier than in my first two years with the Bucks because he's such a tremendous ball-handler and passer. I don't have the ball that much now, but I make it a point to work even harder at getting open. All of us know that if we get open, Oscar will get the ball to us. It's beautiful to watch us play when we're really grooving. Oscar will start the play—looking for his shot or passing in to Kareem inside. Kareem will take one of those unstoppable shots of his, or he'll see me open and pass to me for my set. If I don't have a shot, I pass it back to Oscar, and we start something else. There's nothing radical about these simple options—just basic basketball. It was enough to make us world champions, which I think is a good testimonial to simplicity.

Kareem Abdul-Jabbar, 7-foot-2, 240 pounds, unselfish, clever, intense competitor, has been a winner from Power Memorial Academy in New York City to UCLA to the NBA. He does things on the basketball court that other centers try to do, but there is no one in the history of the game who does them in so awesomely unstoppable a way. He is an orthodox pivot man, you might say, but it seems foolish to say that he plays pivot in an orthodox way.

Kareem Abdul-Jabbar

People who believe I should be able to score points for the Milwaukee Bucks whenever I want to are unaware, unfortunately, of how hard a man has to work to make hard things look easy. It may not seem that I need much energy or agility to shoot the little hooks and jumps and slap shots I use, but that's not true. Believe me, there's nothing easy about hitting a shot when a 300-pounder like Wilt Chamberlain is pushing against you. When you bump into a man like Wilt or Nate Thurmond or Willis Reed in a scramble after a rebound or when you're trying to shoot, neither of you wearing pads, you feel it. You keep feeling it for a couple of days afterward, too!

My height is an advantage to me on the court, but not so much as most fans seem to think. I believe that a center has more responsibility on a basketball team than any other player, to start with. You're the biggest, so you're supposed to score the most points. You're also supposed to do the most rebounding, the most screening for your teammates, and another job you have is to keep plays moving with your passing. A center in the NBA can't be taking attention from the game to look up in the stands for pretty girls, that's for sure.

A difference between the shots a center takes and the shots a guard or forward takes is that you start with your back to the basket. They have their target in front of them; you've got it in back of you. There are two basic areas a center starts from. He can set up at *low post,* which I prefer, or at *high post,* which a center such as Willis Reed prefers. Low post is close to the basket, just outside the 3-second area and on either side of the basket. High post is farther out, usually in the top of the free-throw circle. The shots you try to take and the responsibilities you have on plays depend on which of these two positions you take, and you take the position either out of personal choice or because that's where you belong on certain planned plays.

High-post centers are usually guys with fairly good outside shots facing the basket. They usually are good passers too, and their teammates are often very quick men, clever drivers. High-post centers are able to shoot outside, or work pivot plays with men running past them to be set up or screened for shots. Guys like me who are extra tall, who have good moves and are accurate from short range, generally prefer to set up in low post, so that we're close to the basket both for shots and for rebounds.

The tough thing about being a center is that you can never let up. Even when someone else on your team has the ball, you're working hard at trying to get to the places on the floor from which you're the most dangerous. Other teams know that I'm pretty hard to keep from scoring once I start my shot. It stands to reason they would try to keep my point totals down by forcing me—in very physical ways—away from where I want to be on the court. The tug-of-war situations that take place between centers—the defender with his forearm and elbow and sometimes even his shoulder in the offensive center's back, both of them pushing as hard as they can—are wars for position.

Assume that I've gotten my good low-post position and that Oscar Robertson or Jon McGlocklin or one of our other players has lobbed or zinged a pass to me. Let's also assume that it's in the middle of the second period of a game, with no special situations such as foul trouble or time running out on the 24-second clock. The first thing I do is make sure where I am on the floor. Remember, my back is to the basket, so even knowing where you are is a trick. I gauge my distance from the out-of-bounds lines and also look down at the floor to see what markings I'm near. If I can just

Kareem Abdul-Jabbar's left arm protects the ball from Golden State Warrior Nate Thurmond, and his right arm, fully extended, provides guidance and power as he launches basketball's most devastating shot—his right-handed hook from short range.

reach up to dunk, that's first choice—the surest basket possible. If I'm farther away, I'll look to pass to an open man. My last thought is to shoot, but if that's what the situation says to do, I won't hesitate. My most effective shot is my right-handed hook, so I usually set up on the left of the key. In my basic stance with the ball, it's up high anyway, in position to shoot or pass and also where I can get best grip on it to keep it from being slapped away from me. I swing around on my left or pivot foot and extend the ball with my right hand, using my left to guide and support the ball. The shot is a sweeping, full motion with plenty of wrist-snap and follow-through. As I shoot, I turn a full 180 degrees so that, as I let the ball go, I wind up facing the basket, toward the middle of the floor, and in position to go after the possible rebound. There doesn't have to be a lot of power behind the shot, but you have to concentrate on keeping your balance as guys bump you, and you have to keep it smooth.

Other centers in the league are aware that I'm best with my right hand, so they'll usually try to bump me and push me and pressure me in the other direction. If I were as strong as Wilt or Willis, I'd try to muscle through guys, match my strength against strength. I'm not a bull like them, though, so I try to use finesse— spin off the point of pressure, maybe revolve completely so that I'm facing the basket for a jumper or little dink shot. Maybe I'll use my left hand instead of my right for a hook shot, reversing all the details of mechanics that I need for my normal right-handed shot (you better believe it took a few hours in the gym learning that!). Either way, smoothness, body balance, and full follow-through are things I make sure to remember.

At high post, a center's shot selection is quite a bit different—but not so much different from any other player's. The basic pivot play is the one where you get the pass and one or two teammates run past or *cut* past you toward the hoop. You pass to them either with a bounce behind your back or by turning and hitting them over-hand—if they're open. If not, you either shoot from there or take the drive yourself.

Keeping in mind all the options and jobs a center has in basket-ball—not to mention remembering all the game and foul situations —keeps a guy busy. As I said to start with, you'd better not mind responsibility—not if you intend to make a living playing center in the NBA.

When Dick Van Arsdale of the Phoenix Suns goes into his high gear and comes pounding toward the basket on a drive, fainthearted fans cover their eyes and gore-loving ones get the same eager look that's displayed by aquarium visitors at shark-feeding time. The 6-foot-5 ex-Indiana U star (and his identical twin brother, Tom, of Kansas City, too) is a slashing driver from either a guard or forward position. He's made reckless abandon a standard feature of his game rather than an occasional necessity, demonstrating will to win that makes him not only a team leader but also an exciting player to follow.

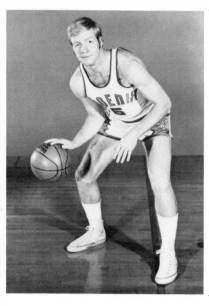

Dick Van Arsdale

Every time I start my move toward the basket to attempt to score a field goal for the Phoenix Suns, a scene flashes into my memory from the Saturday afternoons my twin brother, Tom, and I used to spend in our neighborhood movie house. We loved Westerns when we were kids, and one of our all-time favorite flicks had a scene in it when the hero had to prove his bravery to a tribe of hostile Indians so they'd spare a little group of settlers down in the valley. They offered to let him run the gantlet, and they would spare the folks if the cowboy survived. They made him sprint down a lane between two lines of their meanest, toughest braves while they swung at him with their war clubs, knives, lances, fists—you name it. The hero made it, I remember, but, boy, was he a bloody mess!

Trying to make a layup in a closing moment of an NBA game can be as dangerous and painful as trying to run an Indian gantlet, but a player doesn't dare flinch or cringe or fear to make the attempt—unless he's ready to look for another line of work. Making layups, no matter how tight the opening, is just something every pro must do. Defensive players whack at you and at the ball as you move past them, and often, if you get past the first line of defense, there will be a giant like Wilt Chamberlain or Nate Thurmond under the basket sort of grinning at you and ready to swat you down like a pesky mosquito. You try to out-quick and out-slick the defense to make the shot. Once the ball has left your hands, the congestion works in your favor because the referee will call *goal tending* and automatically award you two points if a defensive player knocks the ball away from the hoop on its downward flight. Even if you're slightly off-target, it's still a possible score if the ball is pinned against any part of the backboard in a simultaneous meeting of ball, board, and defensive hand.

The drive is a good play to try to make for another reason—it can be worth 3 points instead of just 2 if you're fouled on your shot, make it anyway, then sink a free throw. Even when you miss, the percentages are still in your favor because you're likely to be fouled more often on drive plays than when you take any other type of shot from any place else on the court.

The mechanics of the drive are simpler than the theory behind the shot. The ability to dribble well, without looking down at the ball, is a must, and you've also got to be reasonably sure you're a step or two quicker than the man guarding you. If he's playing you tight, you can scoot around him with a fake; if he's playing back away from you, he's got the chance of stopping you because he has a good angle of pursuit. But if he plays back, you can try to hit the outside shot. On the dribble, keep the ball on the side of your body away from the defense and head for the open side of the basket —preferably the side of your strong hand (right, in my case). You jump off your opposite foot (my left, if I use my right hand), and you should be trying to go straight up toward the basket, banking the ball as softly as you can off the backboard to score with an underhand scooping motion of the hand and arm. The most frequent mistakes players make, even the pros, is to jump too soon and waste their power. Have you ever seen a guy come in all alone on a breakaway, take off from the free-throw line—and wind up bouncing the ball off the front rim? It's humiliating. What you should be doing is high jumping, not broad jumping, even though it's more spectacular when players take off from just past the free-throw line and fly through the air. Some coaches feel the ball should be dropped over the front rim, that you should drive straight up the middle if possible. My opinion is that the side approach is better, that the ball should be banked if possible so that you're able to "kill" the momentum of your body and put the ball up softly.

When there are several men clustered around the basket, layups are much more difficult to complete successfully. A jump straight up instead of sideways is even more important in a crowd, because there's a danger of being charged with an offensive foul. At the top of the jump, usually you'll have to release the ball with more force to get it into the basket, and you do this by keeping your hand on top of and behind the ball for more power.

Players about my size who have to make up with aggressiveness and daring for their lack of height justify their reckless-abandon style by using the same line that little boxers used to get: "The bigger they are, the harder they fall." I've got bruises and X-rays that prove another thing: "The smaller they are, the farther they bounce!"

The free spirits of pro basketball are the forwards, permitted to roam out to the deeper areas of the court where guards usually work, yet big enough and close enough to infringe on the centers' favorite territories. Another member of the Phoenix Suns, Connie Hawkins, is considered the most explosive offensive cornerman in the NBA today, succeeding in that role the great Elgin Baylor, former star of the Los Angeles Lakers. Hawkins, an all-time New York schoolyards star who played only his freshman season of college ball, stands close to 6-foot-9 and weighs no more than 215 pounds. But he's durable as steel wire and more spectacular than a Fourth of July skyrocket.

Connie Hawkins

"Do as I say, not as I do," I ought to explain first if I'm to go into the shots I believe a forward needs to play effectively in the NBA. My personal style is more flashy than I would encourage any player of mine to use if I ever went into coaching. Nature was good to me in terms of physical tools. I'm fortunate to be big and also quite quick. Most players are either one or the other. I'm also fortunate to have unusually large hands, which make it possible for me to hold a ball in one hand—and not only to hold it, to manipulate it and work it effectively that way. Of all the players in the NBA, I think only Wilt Chamberlain, Kareem Abdul-Jabbar, and I consistently handle the ball with one hand, which gives us definite advantages.

In my own case, handling the ball easily permits me to do very unorthodox things offensively—little tricks and things which, I have to admit, I enjoy using as part of my fun in basketball, but, more important, little tricks which help my team. Take the usual offensive-defensive situation—me with the ball, trying to score a basket while a defensive man tries to stop me. Like Jerry West, Billy Cunningham, and players like them, I have the self-confidence that I can hipper-dipper my man, give him a quick move left and a quick move right, toss a hip or a toe at him—fake him into committing himself in the wrong direction, in other words, so that I'm free momentarily, which is all the time an NBA player needs, either to go up for a jump shot or to drive for the layup. Being able to hande the ball in one hand is an obvious plus, because I'm able to swoop it, fake passes, fake a jump, and get shooting or driving room more often than other players, who need both hands to protect or maneuver the ball.

Three things help me earn shooting chances. First, I've worked at becoming a good dribbler, shooter, passer, ball-handler. I've also worked on footwork. These are areas of the game that give big men trouble, just as dunking and rebounding are problems for smaller guys. Lack of these skills often is what keeps guys who played center in college from making it in the pros, because they can't adjust to playing new positions. Second, I try to *save my dribble,* so that I can make full use of that ability. And this is a point to remember, no matter what position you play. Saving your dribble means that you make sure you have something definite in mind when you've got the ball—that you head for a particular place on the floor rather than just move at random. It's necessary to protect the ball with your body, but keep dribbling until you get to your destination because, once you stop your dribble, you're not permitted under the rules to start up again. I try to use my dribble to get closer to the basket—*penetrate*—or to where I can take the shot I want to take, or else make as quick and safe a pass as I can. Third, concerning shooting, is that I try to decide instantly, as soon as I get the ball, what I'm going to try to do—and then do that thing immediately. If you wait a second and let your defensive man get position on you, you find he's cut down your choices of what to do. If you get the ball and do something *now,* though, lots of times you can get 2 points before your defender even blinks.

As a forward, I look at my job first as getting points, second as rebounding, and third as defense, with the big emphasis in my particular case on scoring. I'm free to move around the court rather than stay in one area, like a center, and I've learned I'm accurate with my outside shot to around 23 feet or so—deeper than most other cornermen. I usually start my play by looking for the quick, open shot if my man is playing back off me, then either passing or driving if he comes up tight on me. I try to go straight up with my jumper or my set shot, using all my height and concentrating on keeping my elbow close to my body, underneath the ball and in line with the basket. When I drive, I try to ignore my size, you might say. I try to keep low for balance—technically, what you're doing is lowering your center of gravity, which makes keeping your balance easier—and also try to avoid high, slow dribbling because the ball is easier to steal that way. Then, close as I can get to the hoop, I go straight up for the dunk or for the scoop layup.

By being able to handle the ball in one hand, I've been able to time my drive according to whether I've got a clear path to the basket or whether there's somebody in my way. If the lane is clear, I just go straight in. If there's a defensive player waiting for me, I sometimes can make the shot by holding on to the ball longer— delaying—and then dunking or banking the ball off the board from a new angle. My "second chance" at a second angle comes from throwing an extra fake or two at my man. I try, at the same time, to avoid getting too fancy, because it's tough to avoid running into the defender. If the referee rules that he had his position before I started toward him, it's not a field goal—it's an offensive charging foul on me, and the other team gets the ball.

I get paid by the Suns for points, rebounds, and win-loss statistics, not for committing fouls.

Another of the fine forwards in pro basketball is Jack Marin of the Houston Rockets, a 6-foot-6 former Duke University All-American who is regarded not only as an outstanding player mechanically but also as a fierce competitor. Marin is one of the NBA's most accurate and consistent free-throw shooters—an ability which is tiresome to perfect, but which is vital for victories and a torment to those who haven't mastered its simplicity.

Jack Marin

When it comes to shooting free throws, I never miss.

That is, I keep myself thinking I can't miss, because shooting free throws, more than anything else, is being able to step up to the line confident, relaxed, and calm. The trick is to get a groove that feels right, then to practice and practice until you can do exactly the same things every time you step up there and just know the ball's going right into the hoop.

A trick I've learned is to take advantage of as much breather time as I can before I start to shoot. The referee allows you 10 seconds in which to shoot, once he tosses you the ball, but I try to keep away from the line, keep away from accepting the ball, until I catch my breath. An extra 5 or 10 seconds to get yourself together after being slammed to the floor trying to make a layup can make all the difference in the world, especially late in a game. I'll usually take a few deep, deep breaths after I'm fouled on a play, then step to the line when I'm ready, and wait for the ref to give me the ball. Like most players seem to do, I'll bounce it a few times to get the feel of it, then look up at my target, get my concentration going so I hardly hear the roar of the crowd—and zing! One point for my side.

I use the same left-handed set shot for my free throws that I use for set shots during the rest of a game, trying for a fluid, rhythmic motion and trying to do everything exactly the same every time I shoot. Most players nowadays use a one-handed set shot for their free throws, which is a bonus in a way because that's a shot you use in a game, and when you practice free throws you're practicing a game shot—and vice versa. Lots of players used to shoot free throws two-handed—like the old-fashioned two-handed set shots, while still others preferred to shoot with both hands, underhand, a technique that's another part of basketball's early years. Hal Greer of the 76ers is famous for shooting his free throws with the same jump shot he used to pile up thousands of points in a great career. The rule says you must be behind the free-throw line when you shoot—it doesn't say you can't shoot from way, way behind it as Wilt Chamberlain does nor does it say a player can't stand way to one side of the line, like Bob Boozer used to do because he found that the best angle of shot for him.

You can't stress too much how self-confidence and concentration are keys to being a consistently high-percentage free-throw shooter. You can add getting into a groove to the list of musts, too.

Wilt is an example of what I'm talking about. Unfortunately for him, it's a negative one.

There's not a player in the NBA who's not just awed by the things Wilt does on a basketball floor. He's simply overwhelming. Pros wince in sympathy for him, though, every time he has to shoot free throws. Since he holds the NBA record for most free throws attempted, that's a huge number of winces.

Wilt has tried about every style possible in his career: overhand, underhand, one hand, on the line, behind the line—name it. Laker teammates of his tell me that Wilt makes free throws as consistently as an 85-per-center in practice, but that in games he seldom used to shoot any two in a row exactly the same way. Wilt is the first guy to joke about his free-throw-shooting troubles, so please don't think I'm picking on him; he's one guy nobody in his right mind cares to feud with. Since Wilt does joke about his free-throw shooting and since his lifetime percentage is so low, he apparently doesn't have much self-confidence when he goes to the line—and that's one reason, compounding his problem, he so seldom connects.

A few years ago, I remember, Wilt made two free throws in a

row with about 15 seconds left in overtime, to give the Lakers a big, big playoff-game win by two points over Atlanta. Jack Kent Cooke, the dynamic owner of the Lakers, strode into the dressing room after the game wearing a broad smile because his club had won such an exciting game in such a thrilling way. "I had absolute confidence that you would make those two free throws, my friend," Mr. Cooke told Wilt, pumping his hand in congratulations. "I'm glad you had that confidence," Wilt responded, perspiration rolling off his forehead like it does with him, "because I sure as anything didn't!"

4

IF AT FIRST YOU DON'T SUCCEED . . . GET THE REBOUND AND TRY AGAIN

Less than half of all field-goal attempts in a typical NBA game are successful ones, and these are the shots recorded on the scoreboard. The errant shots, bouncing frustratingly off the rim or off the backboards, however, play an even more important role than the bull's-eyes in determining a game's final outcome.

Wilt Chamberlain of the Los Angeles Lakers, the most physically overwhelming player in the history of basketball as well as the most controversial, regards rebounding as more critical to a team than its shooting percentages, and as not only the all-time NBA rebound leader, but also the all-time scoring champion, he is in a unique position to defend that view.

Wilt Chamberlain

The numbers make the story. Every rebound a team gets is worth, I figure, up to 6 points. Most games are won or lost by fewer points than that, so if you have to risk some bumps and bruises going after a missed shot, I say it's worth it.

If a shot hits, it's 2 points. If a shot misses, the offense has the chance to get the ball back so it can work for another attempt. A man may be fouled shooting and, if he is, gets the opportunity for a 3-point play if he can sink his free throw. Rebounding situations, rough as they are, often wind up with a foul call as well as a hoop. Now, if the *defense* gets the rebound, it's another story. The ball goes to the other end of the floor, and the second team gets the chance for the 2 or 3 points.

The difference between 3 points one way and 3 the other is 6 by any math you can come up with.

More than just scoring, rebounding affects other keys to a game, too. If a team is weak in shooting, weak in defense, not stocked with quick players, it still has a chance to be a winner if it can do a job rebounding. A team that does lots of things well but can't hold its own on the boards will be a loser.

Let's talk first about shooting. If a team doesn't hit a high percentage of its shots, it can still roll up big scores if it can rebound its misses and keep shooting—three and four chances at a time—until the ball finally goes in. Boston's series of world-championship teams never were up there in the team shooting percentages, but they were always one of the league leaders in shots attempted and total points scored. In 1966–67, to give another example, I played with the Philadelphia 76ers team which set the record at the time for most wins in a season, 68 (which the Lakers beat in 1971–72 with 69). On that team's front line with me were 6-foot-9 Luke Jackson, 6-foot-6 Chet Walker, and, coming off the bench, 6-foot-6 Billy Cunningham. I can remember lots of nights our shooting wasn't real sharp by pro standards, but I'd go after the offensive rebounds, and ones I couldn't get either Jackson or Walker or Cunningham often could. Whoever got the rebound could shoot again or pitch the ball back out to our guards, and we'd get another chance. What we lacked in accuracy those nights we could usually make up for with persistence.

Rebounding has to be part of your defensive thinking, too. Teams that played the 76er club would, naturally, play the best defense they could, but they still weren't able to shut off our shooting. No defense can prevent pros from shooting altogether. But our opponents couldn't stop us from scoring unless they also got the rebounds on our missed attempts.

Tempo is another thing that works into the winning and losing of games, and tempo is controlled by the team with the ball. If you can dominate the rebounding, you can play at the best pace for your team. You can work patiently for the easy shot or you can helter-skelter and fire just about at will. If you get the rebounds, you can decide whether to go for the fast break or whether to slow things up. You play it according to your personnel and the game situation, and I've had experience both ways.

The San Francisco Warriors team of 1964–65, which won a division championship, didn't have too many quick players, but we had myself, 6-foot-11 Nate Thurmond (who was a rookie then, and playing forward), and 6-foot-7 Tom Meschery up front for rebounding. We were a deliberate team, and we could play it our way because of our strong boards game. The Los Angeles Lakers teams I've played with under Bill Sharman have had a different look altogether, although our results have been equally successful. On that Warriors team, I'd set up in the low post and we'd

Wilt Chamberlain outjumps Warrior Nate Thurmond for the rebound.

get ourselves into offensive position; the ball usually would come in to me, and we'd grind until we had a good shot. With the Lakers, a smaller, quicker team, our idea is to fast break every chance we have and to take the shot even though there may not be anyone downcourt except the shooter himself to go after a miss— something that's supposed to be a basketball sin. I worked exactly the same way going after rebounds with the Warriors and 76ers teams as I do with the Lakers, but Los Angeles players are more running-game conscious. We look for the long pass and the easy shot and only go to our grind-it-out offense when we must. When New York hit so well in the opening game of the 1971–72 playoffs against us, our offense was as hurt as our defense.

It's been an aggravation to me that there's been stuff about "the New Wilt" so often in my career, first in San Francisco, then in Philly, and then in L.A. That 33-game win streak the Lakers rolled up put us in about every newspaper and magazine in the country, I think, except *National Geographic*. Shoot, I was playing just like I always had—fundamental basketball, doing whatever I thought my team needed at a given time in a given game for us to win. The thing that was different from earlier seasons wasn't the way *I* was playing, but what the *rest* of my teammates were doing. Throwing a quick pass doesn't make it if there's nobody down the floor to catch it. Everybody runs in the Lakers' game, and rebounding is the key to a running offense.

One thing about winning 33 in a row, or at least winning most of the time, is that little aggravations don't get to a team the way they do when you lose. A player might leave a wet towel on somebody's chair in the locker room, for instance, and if you're a winner, nobody says anything about it. On a loser, maybe the "victim" chews out the careless guy, and he'll yell back. Pretty soon the sports pages are full of stories about dissension. I've been involved in happy situations and in losing ones. I like to be happy, so I work hard at winning. It's as simple as that.

Wes Unseld of the Baltimore Bullets seems not so much a human being as an invincible steel robot, constructed to perform heavy physical labor and disguised by a layer of flesh so that observers won't be terrified. The chest is massive, the thighs and calves are immense, muscles overlap muscles in his arms, torso, and legs.

The former Louisville University All-American is not only an awesome physical specimen but also a landmark performer in the NBA. At actually less than his officially listed 6-foot-7½ height, he was the smallest starting center in the NBA, and remains the league's finest fast break-igniting rebounder. Unseld proves that strength, unusual quickness for a man of 250 pounds, and unflagging determination can be compensations for lack of height as forward and center for the Bullets, interchanging defensively and offensively with trade-acquired Elvin Hayes.

Wes Unseld

People around the NBA like to say that the Baltimore Bullets play on a 50-foot court. I smile when I hear or read that, because it's proof I'm doing what I do best to help make us a contender.

The Bullets are quick, not big. That's obvious. I'd be playing forward instead of center otherwise. We have to rely on our running game, and the most important ingredient in it, for me, is to get the defensive rebound and pass it down the court as quickly, accurately, safely, and far as I can to one of our other players. We try to get the ball to one of our guards at least *near* the halfcourt line, but if the pass can go full court, so much the better. If we can get a layup or quick jump shot before the defense gets back to stop us and force us into our set offense, our lack of size is less of a handicap than if we have to play at pittypat pace. Since I concentrate so much on getting the defensive rebound and passing long and quickly, we actually *do* seem often to start our plays at midcourt. That's why there's that talk about our playing on a 50-foot court, and I like that.

I wish there were some little thing I do with my hands or feet or body to reveal here as a secret to effective defensive rebounding. There isn't any secret, though, and there aren't any shortcuts, either. It's a matter of working yourself into good rebounding position, working at jumping high and jumping at the right time, and then working at making the good pass. *Work* is the key word. I perspire away maybe six or seven pounds a night doing what I do, and I try to take care of my physical conditioning. You've got to be fit if you're going to be able to be around to be a factor in the last five minutes of eighty-two games a season.

My job begins when the other team has the ball. First, my responsibility is playing man-to-man defense against the other team's center. I have to use my weight and work extra hard at getting good position because I'm shorter than every center I play against. I try to keep between my man and the basket, which just about automatically means that, when a shot is attempted, I'm closer to the hoop than the man I'm playing. That's a plus. But I'm also facing away from the basket when shots are attempted, and that's a minus. So, the first thing I do is turn around while the ball is still up in the air, face the basket, and, at the same time, try to coil down in a semi-squat, elbows sort of wide. This is the position to jump from, and I'm taking up lots of room, so that the offensive center has a tough time trying to get around me. I'll shift with him, jockeying in the process of *boxing out* (it's also called *screening off the boards* and *checking a man off the boards,* and it's a vital skill for all players to master). The idea is that you want to give yourself the best chance you can to get the rebound, but keep your opponent from getting it by keeping him away from the backboard and away from the ball.

I've learned to time my jump so that I'm at the top just as the ball comes down off the backboard or off the rim. That way, I can get both hands on the ball and make my *outlet pass* to one of my teammates to start the fast break. By keeping my hands at shoulder height, palms toward the basket, I keep myself ready to grab a ball coming off at an awkward angle and I have the chance, too, to bring the ball close to my chest, about chin-high, as I grab it so that other players can't slap it away from me. I may be strong, but there are lots of other strong guys in the league too, and you've got to protect the ball on the way down. Two other things I try to do are keep myself from being forced too far under the basket in all the pushing and banging around that takes place when four or five guys go up for the ball, and assume that every shot taken is going to miss.

If I get my hands on the ball, my job is still only half done. I've at least kept the offense from getting a second or third shot attempt, and the Bullets are already ahead of the game, but the next thing is to turn our small advantage into a big one—to turn the rebound into a field goal by getting our fast break started.

This may come as a surprise to most fans—I start my outlet pass even before I ever get up in the air for a rebound, even before the shot is taken! It's a teamwork thing. As I turn toward the basket and screen out my man when the shot goes up, I glance real quick toward both sides of the court to see where the other Bullets are and what they're doing. Our guards will be flaring toward the sidelines, about halfway between the free-throw line and the halfcourt stripe, and our forwards will be heading toward the basket. It's something I do now instinctively, and I've learned to get a good mental picture of just where everybody is, even though I have just a split second to do it. If I get up there at the right time and place and have the rebound, I have a pretty good idea where my guards are, and I can half-turn one way or the other, spot them, and whip a pass to them all in one motion. If everything goes exactly my way, I've made my pass and we've got a man in the clear for a breakaway layup even before I've landed back down on the floor. If I had to get the ball, look for my outlet man, and *then* make my pass, the extra split seconds might be all that the defense would need to stop us.

The defensive rebounder becomes an offensive player as soon he gets his pass made. My assignment after I make my pass is to run on down the floor, about three-quarter speed or so. I'm the *trailer* on the fast break, so I'm back there like a safety man on a football team in case we lose the ball and the other team starts a break of its own. Coming down at not quite full speed, I also may find I'm wide open for an outside jump shot if we miss getting the layup, and with my forward momentum I have a chance to crash through to the boards for an offensive tip-in should somebody shoot and miss.

Some nights it's hard to decide whether it's a blessing or a frustration to be on a team working the fast break like we do. I get sometimes so I feel I'm spending all night running up and down the floor behind the fast break only to find, when I get down there, that Archie Clark or Elvin Hayes or Phil Chenier or somebody has already taken a shot and the ball is already dropping through the net. I turn around and sprint back to where I just came from, because now we're back on defense and I'm right back where I started from.

It's like commuting to an office every morning, running to catch the train and always getting to the depot just as it chugs down the track without you. A guy's got to be a little bit psycho to do this over and over again for 48 minutes a night—and also dedicated to doing a job. Fortunately, I'm both.

Elvin Hayes of the Baltimore Bullets is another of the NBA's leading rebounders and, like teammate Unseld, a star at his position despite his relative lack of height at 6-foot-9. Where Unseld uses his weight and his massive physique to compensate, Hayes, a slimmer man at 230 pounds, uses quickness and jumping ability to combat the giants against whom he must play.

A collegiate star at the University of Houston, following a boyhood in rural Louisiana, Hayes is regarded as one of the most accurate jump-shooters in the NBA, regardless of size or position, and is also an outstanding rebounder.

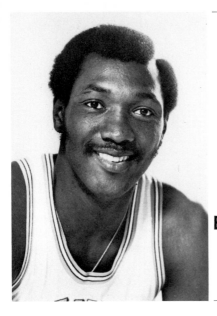

Elvin Hayes

Next time a pro basketball player makes a remark about "the butcher shop," don't look for a bargain sale on pot roast. That's the nickname we have for the area underneath the baskets, where the rebounding action takes place, and the name is a good one, because every time a shot is taken there are going to be hips and elbows and chests and heads flying around, slamming and bumping. During wartime, they say, you can't find any atheists in a foxhole. You don't find many trying for rebounds, either. It's a rough proposition, one of the roughest you'll find anywhere in sports, considering how big and strong guys are in the NBA.

Rebounding happens to be one of the ways I make my living, so it's just something to force myself to tolerate, no matter how many bruises I wind up with. Not only is rebounding painful, it is also loud. There's always the noise of bodies bumping, and some guys grunt and holler extra loud when they go up after a rebound. I think Jerry Lucas of the Knicks is the loudest. You can tell whether he's going to get ten rebounds or thirty by how loud his grunt is when he grabs after a ball against you early in the game.

I think that going after one of your own misses or one of your teammates' misses is easier than going after a defensive rebound.

In offensive rebounding, you're trying to put the ball in the basket, which is something you can accomplish even if you only reach the ball with one hand. In defensive rebounding, you've got to be able to get both hands on the ball and control it enough so that you will be able to make a good outlet pass. Most players jump better off one leg than the other, and in offensive rebounding you can actually add four or five inches to your jump by taking advantage of your stronger leg and sort of leaning that way as you go up. To see what I mean, try standing against a wall and touching as high as you can with both hands at once. Now, try to reach with just one hand, dropping the opposite shoulder. You've added a few inches of reach, right? A one-handed tap has a good chance at success because that's enough control of the ball to get it into the basket.

The harder thing about offensive rebounding, I think, is getting close enough to the backboards and close enough to the ball to take advantage of your "extra" reach in the first place. As an offensive player, I've usually got a defensive man between me and where I want to go when one of my teammates or I shoot. He's trying to box me out, and I don't want to get boxed out, so we start a shoving and faking war. Quickness helps a rebounder because it's better—not to mention less punishing—to step around a man rather than try to out-muscle him.

There's another advantage I have in offensive rebounding that I ought to mention too. Every player's shot reacts a little differently bouncing off the rim or backboard, because every player has a little different spin and arch on the ball when he shoots. I make it a point to start watching my own shots and my teammates' shots as early as our first practice session at fall camp so that I can develop a knack for timing my jumps and being where the ball comes down. Each arena's rims and boards react a little differently— some are tight and some are loose—and you take them into account too, from night to night.

I try to keep my hands up and my palms facing the basket, and I try to reach up and out to sort of caress the ball on my fingertips for a controlled *push* back up toward the basket. I try *not* to slap wildly at the ball, because I have less control of it that way. I also try to keep jumping, a second or third time or even more, because lots of times with several men trying for the ball it keeps up there that long until finally I've put it back in the hole or one of my teammates has made the basket, or until a defensive man takes it down. If I can't get a controlled tip, at least I can try to swat it over to another Bullet, or at least I can keep the ball hopping around for another try. Once in a while an offensive rebounder gets lucky and has a clear shot at a rebound. When that happens for me, I try to get a good two-handed hold on the ball and either go straight back up for a dunk, or, if I don't have that much room, try to pass out to one of my teammates so we can work for another good shot.

When I'm unsuccessful at getting the offensive rebound, I try to prevent the other team from getting a fast break started. I try to wave my arms in front of the rebounder and try to keep him from getting clear passing room for the outlet to one of his guards. I know that it looks a little silly to some fans who don't attend a lot of games to see a man waving his arms and doing what looks like playing defense against a man 90 feet from his basket. I'm not trying to keep him from shooting, which is what it might look like, I'm trying to prevent his making the quick pass out to one of his guards. This tactic is one key thing I have to remember against Nate Thurmond, Wilt Chamberlain, and Dave Cowens—guys who go for the quick, long pass.

All players are tuned in to their personal stats, even though you're supposed to try to keep stats out of your mind. Frontcourt players aren't rated good shooters if they don't hit at least 50 per cent of their shots from the floor. We shoot from closer to the basket, they say, and we get dunks because we're the tallest players. Well, I don't agree with that, because the stats guys charge you with a field-goal attempt every time you make a controlled tap at a loose ball on the offensive boards; they also credit you with a rebound. I say any forward or center who shoots 50 per cent or better earns it, because getting a good tap at the ball with all that beef flying through the air is just as difficult as—and lots more dangerous than —some little guard pumping up a shot from wide open spaces outside.

One of the joys of pro basketball for players, league and team officials, and fans alike is the debut of a collegiate star as a professional. Scouting is so thorough and comprehensive that outstanding players are noticed before they complete their high-school competition, and they are then kept close track of through their collegiate careers as the national public takes note, in anticipation of their eventual eligibility for the draft.

Players like Sidney Wicks come along just once in a great while. A sturdy 225 pounds, Wicks stretches 6-foot-9, yet is more agile and quicker than many guards. He starred on three national championship teams under Coach John Wooden at UCLA and then was drafted by the Portland Trail Blazers for his eagerly anticipated pro debut in the 1971–72 season. Aggressive and intense, Wicks proved himself quickly to be every bit as valuable and spectacular a pro as he had been a collegian.

Sidney Wicks

Moving from college ball at UCLA into the NBA was a huge change for me, sure, but not for the reasons most fans would expect. The pro game is much more physical, and you've got to be a better player to make it in the pros, but the extra roughness and the difference in skills of the pros were things I was prepared for because I've played against pros and done all right against them in summer leagues and in high-school pickup games around the Los Angeles area ever since I was a sophomore in high school. Things that I *did* have to adjust to were the change from a fairly slow tempo in most college games to the fast-break pro pace, and also the difference between playing on three straight national championship teams under Coach Wooden at UCLA and playing for a last-place team in the pros. The tough pro travel schedules and playing even though you may be nursing some minor injury were also hard to get used to at first.

The Trail Blazers are one of the youngest teams in the league, and in my rookie season we had our problems, both on the court and off it. We're learning together, and we'll be better—you can bank on that. But, as a rookie, it was tough for me. Maybe the biggest thing of all I had to adjust to was that the ball seemed to be moving from one end of the floor to the other so often I sometimes had trouble keeping up with it, fast as I am. Because we were a young team, we made more ball-control errors than an experienced team would make, but we also had the energy to play a lot of pressing defenses which forced our opponents into lots of mistakes, too. Games were usually pretty wild at both ends of the court, you see.

My style of play as I came to the pros was to do lots of shooting outside, because, with my height and jumping, not many guys can block my shot, and also to go hard to the backboards for rebounding. Two things I am still learning about pro ball are that I've got to do more driving because defensive players still try to play me very tight, not worrying much about anything except my jumper, and also that a forward's rebounding jobs are different from a center's, even though the mechanical fundamentals are the same.

Forwards generally work farther out from the basket than pivot men, so you can get more of a running start after rebounds. You can get up a little higher with that extra momentum, but you've also got to be careful you don't crash into people already underneath the boards and get called for a foul. You've also got to be careful in jumping to time yourself so you're up there where you can reach the ball at the right time instead of wasting your energy.

Before a forward does anything else about rebounding, he must make sure he's boxing out. Most centers in the NBA are satisfied they'll get their share of rebounds if they're going after them against just the opposite center. If a forward doesn't do a good job of boxing out and his center winds up battling two guys, he's usually in trouble—no matter who he is. Of course, that can be turned around too. Lloyd Neal and LaRue Martin of the Trail Blazers are good shooters and good centers working our offense, but they're not the strongest guys in the league physically. For our team most nights, depending on the man I'm playing against, Lloyd or LaRue will usually work at boxing out on the center and by doing that open things up for me to go for the rebounds against my man. We're reversing what most teams do, but we get results.

A forward also has a decision to make on whether to try for rebounds or to turn to offensive thinking. It depends on your job at a given moment in a game. If your team is doing a good defensive job that night, you can "cheat" a little by first boxing out your man momentarily, then sprinting downcourt as fast as you

Sidney Wicks keeps his palms toward the basket and gets an inside position against Wilt Chamberlain going after a defensive rebound for the Portland Trail Blazers.

can, which pros call *releasing* or *cherry picking*. It means you get down to the offensive area all alone while your defender is back there fighting for the rebound. If a man on your team gets the defensive rebound, he can pass all the way down to you, and you've got a slammer for an easy deuce. Quick, little forwards playing for teams with a big center and a big forward can kill you this way— guys like John Havlicek at Boston, Rick Barry at Golden State, Jim McMillian with the Lakers, and Randy Smith of Buffalo. They tell me Happy Hairston of the Lakers used to get four or five easy baskets a night cherry picking when he played for Cincinnati in the days Wayne Embry and Jerry Lucas were great rebounders for the Royals. With the Lakers, Hairston's job is to help Wilt Chamberlain on the boards because he's the next biggest man on the team. Mc-Millian does the quick releasing now, and Hairston battles against the big guys.

On the other hand, when your team is being out-rebounded in a game, you'll usually have all three of your frontcourt men going after rebounds and boxing out, and sometimes a coach will even tell his guards to chase after their team's missed shots too. When an offensive team *crashes* four or five men to the boards and gets its own rebounds, it will get some extra baskets eventually. But it's dangerous to do, because the other team can have men releasing, and you really set yourself up to be burned.

A forward has to size up the rebounding situation lots of ways, you see, and he also has to be ready to make some quick decisions and switches. You try to watch your center and back him up as much as possible. If he hangs back on defense, protecting against guys breaking loose to the basket and staying ready to block shots, a forward has to see what man the center is ignoring and be ready to pick him up. I'll put that in terms of a typical play in a typical game. Say the Blazers are playing Atlanta and their Lou Hudson is working for a shot from around the top of the free-throw circle. Stan McKenzie, our best defensive guard, or maybe Geoff Petrie, another of our backcourt regulars, is playing defense on Hudson, and probably our center, Lloyd Neal, is playing out from the basket, preventing the Hawks' center, Walt Bellamy, from hitting from outside. If Hudson drives around his man and heads for the basket, Lloyd might slide over, leaving Bellamy and protecting against the drive. When the shot goes up, I know that Bellamy will have a clear access to the boards unless our guard or I try to box him out because we also know that my guy is now out of position to do that job. The play works just the opposite way, of course, if *we* have the ball. If Atlanta neglects to box out Lloyd when one of us drives and Bellamy challenges the driver, then we're going to have a better than normal chance for the rebound.

Since rebounding is so important, you work and work at it. Coach Wooden prepared me for this at UCLA, and I've put lots of the things he preaches to good use in the NBA. What playing at UCLA didn't prepare me for was playing for a losing team. I don't think any player ever gets used to losing, so there's just one possible way to go—I intend to help the Blazers shed their cellar image. I know what it is to play for a winner, know what a satisfaction that is, and I intend to earn that feeling again. One luxury you never get too much of is being a champion.

Jerry West not only gets many compliments, such as the one paid him about his superstar status by Coach Bill Sharman, but also is a man who gives them. "Jerry Sloan," said West in the fall of 1972, "probably plays harder more nights than any other player in the league." From an intense competitor such as West, it was a supreme compliment paid to a rawboned, quiet man from Evansville College in Indiana who has made himself a great pro through hard work and determination rather than through natural physical gifts.

A 6-foot-6, 200-pound college forward, Sloan made the difficult transition to a guard role in pro ball, but his early specialization in rebounding and defense remains a fixture of his game. He is, in fact, regarded as one of the best defensive players and as the best-rebounding backcourt player in all the NBA.

Jerry Sloan

One problem I never had coming to pro ball out of college was accepting being just a member of a team instead of being the star. I've *never* been a star, and I think maybe that's one reason I've been fortunate in my career with first the Baltimore Bullets (1965–66) and then, ever since that rookie season, with the Chicago Bulls. I wasn't considered a *scorer* in college by any means, but I think I was made very aware of possession of the basketball. If I could help our team by being able to get a rebound, that maybe was going to help our club—and that's all I was interested in. That's the way I still play. If you're not a great shooter and you're not one of the guys that can put the ball through the basket all the time, rebounding is something extra that you can do to make yourself helpful, something that may possibly make the coach give you another look and maybe will convince him to keep you on the team.

My rebounding as a guard in the pros also came about because of the type of team the Bulls were back in our first season as an expansion team, before Coach Dick Motta took over our club and we began to climb up in the standings. We weren't very big up front, so I did more rebounding than other teams were used to seeing a guard do. We've got some big guys with us now, and because we have some size, I try to vary what I do rebounding according to the team we're playing against. What we'll sometimes try to do with Bobby Love or Chet Walker playing forward is for me to go to the boards and for them to keep back outside, and this keeps their man from leaving them to try for rebounds. I can go to the boards against maybe a guard who is smaller than I am, and it puts us in a little better over-all rebounding position than we otherwise would be.

My reputation for rebounding is known around the league, and I'm more conscious most of the time of guards trying to box me off the boards than I am of checking them. I should point out, though, that I've played enough at the forward position in my time to know that that's the basic job you have to do first of all, before·you take off. I was taught, if you're not a big person, check the man you're playing and then see what you can do from there.

I look at basketball from a boxing-out standpoint a lot like football. A guy that will block you once may think he has done his job, and, consequently, that isn't always the case. I've gone to the boards many times by the second effort—just having the guy quit on me, and when he does that, I'm able to get to the boards. It's a continuous thing. If you're going to check someone off the boards, you have to maintain that position on the guy until the play is over, until the ball is in somebody's possession.

I've found that I'm more or less a one-handed-type rebounder. I can't jump as high, it seems, if I use two hands. I just don't seem to be high up enough, so I mainly just try to keep the ball alive or, better yet, slap it to a teammate I see that's in the open when I do go up. You can see what's going on, and you try to take advantage of situations. Playing that way, I'm more effective as an offensive rebounder than as a defense boards man, but that also means I've got to really push myself to be ready to get back on defense if we don't get the ball. When I do get the ball after the other team shoots and misses, I do just what any other rebounder does—try to get the ball to the little man, try to get something going. You look downcourt first, because sometimes you can get the ball and throw it the length of the court—and that saves a lot of running. If the fast break isn't there easily, I'll take my time more, because the Bulls aren't a hurry-up team, we're more of a control team. As a guard, I can dribble down to our end if I can get the rebound, or I'll pass it to somebody and we'll go down to set up our offense.

For guards who are what you might call "normal size," 6-foot-2 or so, give or take a few inches, rebounding situations don't call for them to try for the ball, but, depending on how the coach wants to play, to try to head for the sidelines. You'll either start a fast break, if it's defense and the outlet pass is going to come to you, or try to stop it by getting position on the man looking for a pass. Sometimes you can anticipate the pass and intercept it, or at least you can slow a team down and give your defense a chance to get set up. Saving a basket is just as good as making one, I've always been taught. Guards also should be alert when a shot is taken, because lots of times the ball won't bounce straight up in the air where the big guys can go for it. It'll take the long bounce out toward the floor. I try to turn toward the basket when a shot is taken, try to box out somebody, and keep my hands up, in case a long rebound heads in my direction and I'm not all-out crashing.

I have no delusions. I'll never win many one-on-one contests, and I'm definitely not a fancy ball-handler or a dead-eye outside shooter. I work on the things I can do to help my team win basketball games. When you're not a superstar, the best thing to do, I believe, is to try that much harder. If thinking and acting like that makes me sort of an Avis of pro basketball—well, that's the way it'll have to be.

5

IF YOU MUST LOAF,
LOAF ON OFFENSE

When pro basketball people get together after hours, the story gets told of the rookie coach of a team of veterans and just one rookie, a hulking kid from a Southern college who didn't get to play much, but who wanted to make a contribution and who wanted most of all to be accepted by the team. They trailed by two points with ten seconds to go one night, had the ball at midcourt, and called time out to huddle and strategize for a last-gasp, tying-basket attempt. The neophyte coach was caught unprepared. He'd lost his poise and had no attack plan to offer. He looked at his players, huddled around him and panting for breath, and blurted with growing panic, "We gotta get a hoop! We gotta get a hoop! Anybody got an idea?"

The players looked blankly at each other, first stunned at their coach's failure to guide them, and then themselves momentarily bereft of ideas. A time out lasts only sixty seconds, but this one seemed to last an eternity as the players looked blankly at their coach and he looked blankly at them.

The big rookie, eager to please and feeling compelled to contribute in what otherwise was a vacuum of thought, leaned over into the huddle and offered, in drawled, puppy-like eagerness, "Well, when I was back in college, my coach, he always used to tell us, 'The best offense is a good defense!' "

Theoretically accurate and wise as that advice may have been, it wasn't appropriate to that particular situation. Defense in the NBA actually *has* come to be many teams' best offense, but not necessarily with ten seconds to go in a close game.

The Boston Celtics built their long reign as world champions on the foundation of defense developed by their brilliant center, Bill Russell, and subsequent world champions have made strong defense devastating weapons in their conquering arsenals, too. Willis Reed, a product of the same Grambling College of Louisiana which has produced so many pro football stars, captained the New York Knicks to the NBA title in the 1969–70 season. With his 6-foot-10, 240-pound bulk the hub not only of a fine, fluid offense, but also of a pressuring, gambling defense, he helped the Knicks electrify the nation their big year and was voted the NBA's Most Valuable Player.

Willis Reed

Don't look any further than me and my sensitive knees if you need final proof that the idea nobody plays defense in the NBA has been dead for a long time. I watched more games from the bench during the 1971–72 season than I want to remember, in my civvies sitting next to Coach Red Holzman, because I had developed a sore tendon behind my left kneecap. I could have helped the Knicks with my shooting despite that injury, maybe, and I *know* there were a few nights I could have hobbled enough at least to set some picks for our outside shooters, but there was no way I had enough mobility to play defense or could jump well enough to rebound.

What I want to make clear is that defense in the pros is a special thing. The 24-second clock has a tremendous influence on what we can and cannot do, and pro defense also is influenced by the fact that teams play each other fairly often. Of course, pro defense is also much more physical and punishing than in any other kind of ball.

Players who make it in the NBA have so many moves and are such great, quick shooters that trying to keep guys from getting shots doesn't do the job. Except for the closing seconds of a very close game, I mean. Pros are going to get their shots and they're going to get their points, but you can at least try to make the percentages work in your favor.

The 24-second clock makes the difference. Pros don't have to keep guys from shooting. They just have to keep guys from shooting relaxed, comfortable, well-set-up shots and keep them from shooting from their best percentage areas. The new pressuring defenses that the Knicks helped make so popular in the NBA don't prevent teams from getting shots, but they make them use up time before they can shoot. They also make teams take bad shots because they're trying at least to make *some* kind of scoring attempt within the time limit. Since a rushed, off-balance shot or a shot from territory where a player doesn't hit accurately is likely to be a bad one, it's likely to be a miss—and rebounding becomes all that much more important.

It's gotten to the point now that lots of coaches tell their players to work as hard as they can on defense, that if they have to try to pace themselves and save their energy—or downright loaf, if a lead is big enough—to do it on offense by just staying out of a play, but to keep hustling on defense. There's really been a revolution in the league, and this thinking also shows something that pros learn the hard way—that playing defense is mostly a matter of being willing to work hard. If a guy is quick enough and big enough to be a good scorer, he's probably got enough natural physical ability to be a good defensive player. Of course, he's got to be willing to pay the physical price, and he also has to use his brains—study the opposition. You can't keep a guy away from his favorite shooting areas if you don't know where they are.

When you think about how hard teams work to force shooters into doing awkward things and to keep them away from the high-percentage shooting areas, you have to marvel even more about the greatness of the NBA's superstars. They're constantly challenging you physically, challenging you to stop them from doing what they want to do. Oscar Robertson can shoot accurately from any place past halfcourt, it seems, but the guys who have to guard him complain after they've tried to stop him that if he has a 20-foot shot possible, he'll fake them and muscle them and get a 15-footer. If he has a 15-footer, he wants to shoot from 10. I didn't see the series, but they tell me that when Wali Jones, now with Milwaukee, was a rookie with the Baltimore Bullets in the 1965 Western

What Willis Reed may lack in finesse he makes up in determination as he powers through Golden State Warrior Clyde Lee at Madison Square Garden.

Division playoffs, he did a fantastic job crowding Jerry West, staying with Jerry all over the court, not giving him any room to shoot and not conceding an inch. But that also was the series that Jerry averaged close to 50 points a game! It's gotten to the point that players aren't judged great just because they are great shooters, but only if they have Oscar's kind of muscle and moves to get good shots, or Jerry's kind of quickness to get good shots even under extreme pressuring.

We figure that possession of the ball is worth about 1½ points— not quite a field goal. That's based on league-wide shooting percentages and the teams' average number of points per game. It's interesting to consider that team accuracy figures have gone up as individual skill has improved, but that team scores have gone down as clubs concentrate more on team defense. If you can force a bad shot and get the rebound, or if you can steal the ball, intercept a pass, or force a ball-control error, you're more than halfway home to getting a deuce up on the scoreboard, and over the 48 minutes of a game the figures add up.

There's not much more embarrassing to a team than to get the ball and then give it up for one reason or another, either because of its own mistake or because of something the defense does, without at least getting a shot. Losing the ball without getting at least a try for a hoop is called a *turnover*, and one more proof that the league has become defense-conscious in the past dozen years is that turnovers are now listed as a regular feature of the official box score.

You don't hear guys in the dressing rooms talking about how they made a great steal or block on Oscar or Jerry or Earl Monroe or Connie Hawkins yet, but maybe it's just a matter of time. When the stats man comes in to hand out copies of the game sheet, guys still look to see first how many points they had, then how many shots they took and how many they made, but the coaches know who worked on defense and who didn't, and the general managers are taking defense into account when guys come in to talk about their contracts. Ego is one thing, but money's another, so defense absolutely is here to stay.

The work in playing defense involves use of fundamental, physical mechanics as well as cleverness and mental quickness. These are

assets that, along with great offensive ability, have made Dave
Bing of the Detroit Pistons one of the most respected players in the
NBA. When a detached retina forced him to miss most of the early
1971–72 season, the Detroit Pistons sagged so badly that, in unfor-
tunate frustration, Bill van Breda Kolff resigned as coach. Before
selecting Earl Lloyd to succeed van Breda Kolff, the Detroit man-
agement recognized Bing's over-all basketball mastery by asking
him to serve as interim leader of the team. He declined, but the
request was a tribute to the 6-foot-3 former Syracuse University
star's mental as well as physical command of the game.

Dave Bing

Thinking defense has never been a hardship for me. I grew up playing ball in Washington, D.C., where one-on-one games and schoolyard ball are probably the second favorite sport in town—next to the wheeling and dealing that goes on up on Capitol Hill. I was lucky to have good early coaching in fundamentals, and I'm glad I learned my lessons.

Playing defense is more important nowadays in the NBA for me than it might have been if I'd have come into the league ten years ago. Teams *never* would match up their best offensive guard or forward defensively against the other team's best scorer at that position, because offensive stars were supposed to save their energy for scoring and because a key offensive man might get into foul trouble. If I'd come into the NBA ten years ago, I might not ever have had to guard Jerry West or Oscar Robertson, for instance— or maybe not until the final minutes of a real close game, anyway. Now, number-one guards match up against number-one guards all the time. The big-gun forwards haven't had to bang heads too much yet, but I wouldn't be surprised if that becomes a trend before long, too. I understand that Oscar and Jerry match up against each other as the rule instead of the special situation nowadays, and

I've seen them really have some fantastic wars against each other in playoff games.

It's easier playing pro defense because of the 24-second clock and because pros try to force bad shots rather than to shut guys off from shooting altogether, but your fundamentals are the same no matter where you play, even if the thinking is a little different.

Your man can't score and can't shoot if he doesn't have the ball, so that's a first rule of defense no matter what position you play— keep your man from getting the ball. Stay between him and the ball-handler, wave your arms, be alert to prevent free room for someone to pass to him—block the passing lanes.

If he gets the ball—since I'm a guard, playing against guards, my man often will bring the ball downcourt in the first place—then my tactics naturally have to be different, and they'll also be different depending on the guy I'm playing. From past games against him, I'll usually have a good idea whether the guy is a shooter or a passer type, first of all—whether he's going to look first to try to score or whether he's going to try to set somebody else up for a shot. If he *is* a shooter, I have to keep in mind whether he's a player who prefers to drive or whether he prefers to take the outside shot. Another "rating" you must make, or remember, is whether, on the dribble, the man prefers to go to his right or his left. Pros are supposed to be so good they can do everything and go all directions, but the truth is that we all get into set habits. I don't keep all this information written down in a little black book, but some of the guys in the league actually do keep track of the men they have to play against that way, with card files or notebooks. For college teams and even now sometimes in the pros, when coaches want scouting reports, these are things they want to know about individual players.

The rule about this set of choices the offensive man has is that whatever he likes and wants to do, you try to force him to do the opposite. If he's a shooter, you may crowd him and shove him, use your hands on his hips a little, whatever you can to force him to give up the ball. If he's a passer, you might lay back from him and dare him to shoot because you cut off his passing possibilities, waving your hands and harassing him. An outside-shooter type of player needs room, so you crowd him and keep a hand in his face. The driver can be played back, so that you can step in front of him and then stay there. The farther back you're able to stay from him, the easier your job is, because you're cutting down his angle of drive. Think of it as a pie wedge, with the basket in the middle of the pie. When your man dribbles, you'll be able to keep up with him by playing just opposite him and keeping pace with him, but that's not doing enough of your job. You don't want to just keep up, you also want to force him to do what's uncomfortable for him. Instead of playing him nose to nose, you can shade half a step toward where he wants to go, then pressure him with your body in the aggressive, forcing way we call *overplaying*.

Naturally, he's going to be doing everything he knows to do to cancel what you're doing, so you've got to be that much tougher than he is, that much quicker. Footwork is very important. On defense, you try to slide to one side or the other, like a boxer or like a crab, shuffling with quick steps and never, never crossing your feet. You must avoid tripping yourself, which can easily happen if the man fakes one direction and then zips off in the other and you've crossed over. He'll try to shoulder-fake you, fake a pass, fake with his feet, with his eyes—whatever he can to get you off-balance in the wrong direction for even a split second. You're on the alert not to go for the fakes, and the best way I've learned is to watch my man's midsection. No matter what fake he makes, he's not going anywhere without his stomach. Another fake that a number of players like to use is to go up on their toes and lift the ball as though they were going to shoot. They want you to jump with them—and as you do, they can duck under you for the drive or get you out of sync with them—go up for their shot just as you're on the way down from yours. The counteraction the defensive man must take is to avoid leaving his feet until the last possible second. In fact, leaving your feet any time in basketball is a dangerous thing unless you know exactly what you're doing, because once you're in mid-air, you've lost a lot of your ability to control your body.

Pros know all of these fundamental things, know what everybody's moves and habits are, know what different defensive players are going to try to do against them. One man's ability against the other's is what pro defense is all about. Knowing how to stop a man and then actually stopping him is your constant challenge. Every guard in the NBA knows that Jerry West prefers to go to his right for his shot, and everybody overplays him that way, crowding him and giving him as little shooting room as possible because he's so dangerous from outside. But he still gets his 25 or so points a game. Jerry West is a superstar, not just a star, and that ability to get his job done even though defensive men have his moves memorized is one reason he's earned that rare label.

Where guards are able to utilize their quickness and cleverness playing defense in the areas away from the basket, forwards must be strong, durable, big, mean, and tough in order to stymie the offensive stars, who have all of these traits as well as determination to put the ball in the basket.

The NBA cornerman of today who most perfectly fits this ideal is 6-foot-6 Dave DeBusschere of the New York Knicks. He's a fixture not only on all-star teams, but also on all-defensive teams, because of his physical tools and because of his zeal. DeBusschere is unique among NBA players in that he is a former pitcher for the Chicago White Sox as a $60,000 bonus player out of the University of Detroit, a big-league baseball player at the same time he was a big-league basketball star. He was so highly regarded by Pistons owner Fred Zollner in 1964 that, when it came time to select a new leader for the team, he designated DeBusschere as his team's twenty-four-year-old player-coach. The versatile 235-pounder carried that dual burden until the spring of 1967, then was traded to the Knicks in exchange for Walt Bellamy and Howie Komives on December 19, 1968, in a deal regarded as the final, vital element in the Knicks' climb to greatness.

Dave DeBusschere

What? Dave DeBusschere a tough guy? I'm a pussycat compared to some of the men who used to play in the NBA, even though I'm supposed to be pretty rugged. A push here, a shove there, a little nudge with an elbow—they're tools of my trade as the forward for the Knicks who takes the tough defensive assignment every game. I guard Spencer Haywood one night, Connie Hawkins the next, Rick Barry another—and so on and so forth from October to May. Aggressiveness and hard work go into playing these guys, but nobody thinks of me as the Knicks' *policeman*, fortunately for my conscience.

That delicate little phrase used to be almost as standard a way to talk about positions on a pro team as *cornerman, guard*, and *pivot*. The policeman was the bruiser every team had to have to equalize things if his team's star scorer was getting an especially vicious physical going-over from the other team. The policeman, who might or might not be a sound player otherwise, would go into the game and deliver a few well-aimed and well-timed elbows—dish out just enough mayhem to make sure the offending team got the message. If he picked up three or four personal fouls in a hurry, it hardly mattered. "You get six personals," the saying went, "but if you use them right, six is plenty!"

I don't remember policemen *personally*, mind you. I heard about them from the older pros back when I was just breaking into the NBA with Detroit. Games were rough enough at that time, but, I was told, not as rough as they had been in the earlier days. One guy I heard about, a forward—most policemen seemed to be forwards—played defense with his forefinger, and he was murder. As his man went up for a jump shot, this brute would move in close and, when he knew the referee had no angle to call the play, poke out with his index finger into the shooter's solar plexus. He never poked hard enough to maim—just enough to double up his man and send the shot well off the target. Another policeman had the cute habit of keeping his man from rebounding or driving on him by grabbing the waistband of the man's shorts when the referees were screened. This was before the age of the miracle fabrics, though, and that clever little tactic got stopped one night when he held on to his man's pants, the man drove for the hoop—and the pants ripped completely off! I haven't named names so that I can protect the guilty—and also because I want to protect Dave De-Busschere. Policemen's legs go with age, but they never lose their clout.

Roughness by today's pro standards actually is milder than ever because teams are more and more putting a premium on quickness rather than on bulk. Today, there's still a lot of belly-bumping and hipping and use of hands on defense, just as there always has been, but there's no player in the league with a reputation for hurting opponents intentionally.

The judgment most pros like to see referees follow is "no harm, no foul." By that I mean that if it were up to me, there wouldn't be a foul whistled on a play unless contact were deliberately vicious or unless it seriously affected the play. I'll make a confession, though. I argue this philosophy with more conviction when I'm playing defense than when I have the ball myself.

Forwards don't move around on the floor as much as guards do, but I've played some backcourt in my day—came into the NBA that way, actually—and I know that basic mechanics of defense are similar for both positions. I go into a game thinking that a star forward who averages 25 points a game is probably going to get his

Dave DeBusschere, driving past Milwaukee Bucks' Bob Dandridge on his way
to the hoop, shows he knows what to do with a basketball when it's his turn
to take the offensive.

25 on me too, no matter what. Give or take a basket or two. What I want to do by using my body, my hands, and my arms is to make sure that, if my man makes his 25 most nights taking 18 shots from the floor, against me he's going to have to try 30. And I'm going to be taking my licks at the other end of the floor, don't forget. He'll have to worry about stopping me, and I'm willing to take my chances that I'm strong enough and in good enough shape from the way Red Holzman works us that I'll wear him down more than he tires me.

The rule our team follows on defense is "See the ball," an instruction we get from our coach constantly. The trick is to sort of split your vision between the man you're guarding and the ball, a step toward using the fundamental truth that the best way to stop a man from scoring is to keep him from getting the ball. I try to screen him, block off the pass routes to him. The big, strong shooters like Spencer Haywood, Bob Kaufmann, and Sidney Wicks are punishing to play against because you can't wear them out and can't muscle them, but I'd almost rather play them than the quick forwards like Bob Love, Cazzie Russell, and John Havlicek because they're so much more active and because it's harder to keep them from getting the ball. Still, the more difficult a defense makes it for the other team to pass, the more likely it is to force the man with the ball into making a mistake, into some kind of turnover, or at least into taking a shot he doesn't want to take.

The necessity for keeping your man from getting the ball increases as he moves toward the basket. I use my hands on his back or side so that I can keep track of where he is, yet still be able to keep my eye on the ball, and I have to rely on my teammates to yell at me with warnings about picks or screens. If my man *does* squirt past me and toward the basket, I'll make sure to keep my hands up and waving so that I have a chance at deflecting or intercepting a pass aimed for him as he cuts.

In the Knicks' helping, gambling defense I have another type of assignment when Walt Frazier or Earl Monroe tries for a double-team on the guard with the ball. I "cheat" up toward the unprotected man who's been left open, and behind me our center and our other forward have to watch out to leave their men and protect behind me. Our plan is to force that mistake or force the offense to rush the shot so that we've got a chance at a rebound and fast break.

Most NBA teams have a pressure defense in their bag of tricks to use those days when they need something to get them back into a game they've come to trail in badly. Because two men often wind up harassing the man with the ball, these defenses can look like the zone press defenses UCLA used to win all those NCAA championships. More accurately, they're still man-to-man, but borrowing some of the zone's principles.

What you might say is that defense in the less sophisticated NBA days was sort of a cross between ice hockey and checkers—demanding some thinking, but mostly toughness. Today it's more a combination of football pass defense and chess. The difference is that there's less surgery work for the orthopedic specialists now, but more tape to dispense for the trainers.

One of my earliest basketball memories is of a college game I watched on television in Los Angeles. A small Jesuit university team from San Francisco was playing in the tiny gym on the UCLA campus, which was Westwood's only basketball facility until the building of gigantic Pauley Pavilion more than a decade later. It was in December, and the year was 1954, ten years prior to UCLA's first national championship, but five years into the coaching career there of John Wooden, and already the Bruins were a perennial West Coast power. UCLA, led by Willie Naulls, defeated USF, but the then only regionally known losing team center, Bill Russell, played brilliantly. That was the last game Russell ever lost as a collegian. He went on to lead his team to fifty-five straight victories and two NCAA championships, then became the greatest winner in professional history, too.

Russell, even as a college junior and despite the fact he was less than 6-foot-10, had mastered a new play in basketball—the blocked shot. When he became the star of the Boston Celtics, he ignited a professional revolution by singlehandedly affirming the value of suffocating defense. Russell invented what amounted to an entirely new concept of defensive play for centers, thwarting not only his rival pivot man, but virtually challenging all five opposing players simultaneously as well. The blocked shot—or its threat—was Russell's patented weapon.

A generation of NBA centers has followed in Russell's footsteps, beginning with Wilt Chamberlain—in his defensive play more than with his scoring, because Russell only lightly concerned himself with shooting—and continuing to such contemporaries as Elmore Smith of Buffalo, Kareem Abdul-Jabbar of Milwaukee, Rick Roberson of Cleveland, Dave Cowens of Boston, and others. No ranking of NBA stars would be complete without another of the defensive giants of the Russell mold—6-foot-11 Nate Thurmond of the Golden State Warriors, a former Bowling Green University star who is not only one of the league's finest players but also one of its most widely respected and well-liked personally.

Nate Thurmond

There aren't many men as big as I am, 6-foot-11, who come into the NBA as rookies and have to play forward. I'm one of that small group, and the reason was a fellow named Wilt Chamberlain. Wilt was already a five-year superstar when I was drafted by the San Francisco Warriors in 1964, and I played forward alongside him for a year and a half, before he was traded to Philadelphia. I didn't make anybody forget Elgin Baylor the way I played forward, but I learned a tremendous amount about what an NBA center's job is by playing the front line with Wilt before I took over in the pivot myself.

We worked against each other in practice, which was quite an education, considering I weighed only 225 pounds then, and still go only about 235, but the most dramatic lesson Wilt taught me was something that happened in the postseason playoffs in April of '65. He singlehandedly destroyed the St. Louis Hawks in the seventh game of the Western Division finals with three plays late in the fourth period at the Cow Palace in San Francisco, which not only won us the division title but also gave me a model to follow the rest of my career as far as playing defensive center is concerned.

We'd led most of the way, but with about five minutes left St.

Louis was getting some momentum going, and some of us younger
Warriors players began to feel a chill. Richie Guerin, a great guard
who later became the Hawks' coach and, in 1972, their general
manager down in Atlanta, broke loose on a steal and was on his
way to a layup that would have cut our lead to six points. Wilt
overtook him with those giant strides of his. Just as Richie went
up for his shot, my man reached up with that big right hand of
his to swat the ball away. Poor Richie. When Wilt knocked the ball
into the seats, you'd have thought somebody had hit him over the
head with a club, he was so shocked. But the Hawks weren't dis-
couraged yet. We scored, and then St. Louis came down to set up
a medium-range jump shot for its great all-pro forward, Bob Pettit.
Wilt was playing back deep to cut off any drives, but he leaped
out to near the free-throw line to slam the ball practically down
Pettit's throat. We got the loose ball and scored again, but St.
Louis, although staggering, wouldn't play dead. Next time down,
the Hawks' other great forward, Cliff Hagan, faked around me
and was in the clear for a driving layup, but Wilt got over to him
in time once more and made an even more fantastic block on him
than he had on Guerin. A couple of minutes were left to play, but
the Hawks knew they were hopeless after that third block of Wilt's.

That's when I learned blocks do more than just save baskets.
They also give you offensive opportunities and, most important,
can demoralize the other team.

Centers who tried to duplicate the blocks that Bill Russell and
Wilt Chamberlain were making five and six years ago used to try
to use psychology more than centers do today. Russ or Wilt would
go for blocks only six or seven times a game, but the offensive team
never knew *which* six they'd go after. Every player on the teams
they were playing was aware of this. They'd make drastic changes
in their shooting styles, putting exaggerated arch on the ball, and
when they did, it threw off their timing and their rhythm because
they wanted to keep the shot out of reach. Russ and Wilt might
block only a half-dozen, but they'd intimidate five times that many
field-goal attempts, and I adopted a similar technique for myself.

With the new emphasis on defense that's happened in the NBA
the last few years, centers are no longer that conservative. We're
blocking—or at least trying to—as many shots as we can, concentrating harder than ever before on not just stopping the other center, but also shutting off the middle to the other team entirely. In

time, you learn when to try the block, when not to to avoid goal-
tending violations. I want to deny the drive to the team I'm playing
altogether, make them do their shooting from outside, and I'll take
my chances that the Warriors can score enough points to win unless
our opponent shoots fantastically from the perimeters. The block
really has become an offensive weapon, because you're trying to
slam the ball to where one of your teammates can reach it and
start a fast break, not just knock it out of bounds. I may drop off
the center to protect the middle, and if I do it's up to one of my
forwards to help me by boxing out my man off the boards.

One reason I can play that way, or that any center can play
that way if he wants to try, is that we've got the whole floor in front
of us, with the basket behind us. It's something like the edge that
a catcher has on a baseball team, and the similarity goes deeper
because, like a catcher, a basketball center calls the plays. On a
bunt in baseball, say, the catcher will yell for either the third base-
man or the pitcher to make the play, whoever is in better position
for it. Or on a popup the catcher—with the whole field in front
of him—will run out to yell for the player in best position to make
the catch. A basketball center's yelling is to alert his four teammates
for picks and screens. If Jeff Mullins is guarding Pete Maravich,
say, and Pete tries to dribble so that Mullins will run into a pick set
by Walt Bellamy, I'll yell, "Pick left!" or "Pick right!" so Jeff
can either slide around it, or call for me to switch over to Maravich
temporarily while Jeff picks up Bellamy. For Jeff to slide around
Bellamy, staying with his man by *fighting through the pick*, is the
better thing for us because it avoids creating a mismatch.

Lots of chatter goes on during a game, guys yelling out play
numbers to each other and defensive players warning and alerting
each other, but most fans don't know about the yelling unless they're
fortunate enough to sit very close to the floor.

Speaking of yelling, Russell's contributions to basketball were
more than just the emphasis on defense generally and blocking
shots. Another thing he invented—maybe I'd better say it was
invented *for* him—was Boston's famous "Hey, Bill!" defense. With
Russell back there to protect against the drive, Boston's guards
always used to press and overplay their men. When a Celtic got
careless or when an offensive player put a really dazzling move on
his man and left him standing there open-mouthed, the Celtic

would turn and scream, "Hey, Bill!" The amazing thing was that, with Russ playing back there, the "Hey, Bill!" defense often worked.

A play just as demoralizing as the blocked shot is the steal, a technique developed to as fine and delicate an art as pickpocketing. Among the more capable practitioners is 6-foot-2 Archie Clark of the Baltimore Bullets, a former University of Minnesota teammate of Atlanta's Lou Hudson and an all-star guard noted for his scoring and quick-handed defense.

Archie Clark

Guards who live by the steal also can get burned by it, so I know from personal embarrassment how having the ball swiped from you and taken on down the floor for a breakaway basket can momentarily demoralize a player.

The hardest thing in basketball, I think, is to generate a spurt of offense to break a game open. I've played with Los Angeles and Philadelphia at earlier times in my pro career, and it seemed that if those teams broke games open, it was usually with a few steals mixed in with a blocked shot or two. We could score three or four quick baskets, get something going, and pull away. Now that I play with Baltimore, I find that Wes Unseld's quick outlet passes give us a consistent fast break in more orthodox ways, but the steal remains a valuable tool—if used correctly.

I want the man I'm guarding to worry that I might go for the ball, to worry that I might make him look bad. I'll fake digging for the ball a lot, maybe slap at his knees. . . . It's part of the psychological warfare. Before I actually do try for a steal, I think about the foul situation, the score, whether my man is a good free-throw shooter or not, and what my personal foul situation is.

I also try to make sure that, if I try for the steal and don't make it, my man won't be in the clear for an easy hoop.

Naturally, if I've got four or five fouls on me already, I'd be foolish to risk being disqualified by fouling on a steal try. Or maybe I've only got one or two personals, but our team is already in the bonus foul situation. Unless I have a clear shot at a steal, I'm risking giving the offensive two cheap free throws. Sometimes you lay off making a steal early in a game, even though you're sure you could get the ball if you wanted to. Then, late in the game, when it really might mean something and after I've given my man a false feeling of security, I'll zap him good!

The technique isn't complicated. To steal a ball, you keep yourself low, keep your hands up and wide, be ready to move quickly in any direction, anticipate where your man wants to dribble, and then make your move. I never go for the steal try on the downward push of the ball off my man's hand and toward the floor—he's got too good a control then. Instead, I try to get my hand in and on top of the ball as it comes off the floor on its *upward* bounce. I'll try to zip around, pick it up on the move, and go the rest of the way for the layup if I can, but if that's impossible, I try at least to slap the ball over toward one of my teammates so that he can get it.

Caution is needed because some ball-handlers sort of dare you to try for the steal. They'll dribble out farther from the body than the book says they should, and when you lunge for the steal, committing yourself, they'll pull the string and either take the jumper or fake it and drive.

It's a horrible feeling to be bringing the ball up the floor, be looking for your men so that you can set up a play, be dribbling steadily, then—all of a sudden—find you're pushing nothing but air while a man is laughing at you all the way to the other basket. If I have my choice, I prefer to be the laugher rather than the guy who's being humiliated.

6

SPECIAL STROKES FOR
SPECIAL FOLKS

"Hot dog!" There aren't many labels a basketball player wants to avoid as urgently as that one, reserved for the player who attempts to glorify himself by making what ought to be a simple play look difficult. There are times when a wraparound, behind-the-back pass is the only way to make a play, and there are times when dribbling aimlessly over the floor to run out the clock is the correct thing to do, but more commonly the objective of the polished professional is to make every play in the simplest, surest way possible.

Passing, moving without the ball, coping with or establishing mismatch situations, making the play, setting up an offensive situation —these are areas with potential for flamboyance. The cool veteran sets out to accomplish these plays as steps toward victory, not toward ego gratification. Individual styles of the pros build in the spectacular, and the experienced fan recognizes when a play is made for the sake of victory or for the mere sake of needless showmanship.

Among the dedicated pros is Gail Goodrich of the Los Angeles Lakers, another of John Wooden's UCLA products, and, at barely 6 feet tall, one of the smallest players ever to find a niche in a season's list of top ten scorers. He played a vital role in the Lakers' 1971–72 world championship with his accurate shooting, but made just as great a contribution to the team's cascade of victories with his passing, ball-handling, and general hustle.

Gail Goodrich

I can hardly remember a time I haven't had a basketball in my hands, haven't been intensely wrapped up in the game. My dad, Gail Goodrich, Sr., was captain of the team at the University of Southern California in 1935, and it was just something I grew up with—a game to play and also a game to read about, even before I entered serious competition in high-school ball—long before I ever decided to go to UCLA.

In all the basketball textbooks I remember reading, there always seemed to be pages and pages of diagrams and explanations of how to throw the *shovel pass*, the *overhand pass*, the *baseball pass*, the *bounce pass*, the *two-handed snap chest pass*—names I've hardly ever heard any of my teammates use and names I've seldom used myself. A player doesn't come down the court and think, "Hey, there's an open man. I think I'll throw him a *two-handed bounce pass with reverse English.*" You see the man and you pass, that's all. Passing is the quickest way to move the ball—that's the key thing. You rely on your instincts, and if you have to stop to think, you might as well forget it, because, by the time you've made your decision, the opening probably has been closed.

At that, passing takes a good partnership. A completed pass

means somebody throwing and somebody else catching, and both men have their responsibilities, both before and after the pass is thrown.

Only one offensive player at a time can have the ball. The four other men ought to be moving—because they're either running a set play or in free-lance movement. Otherwise, it's the simplest thing in the world for a defense to close the passing lanes and force the ball-handler into making a mistake. When you see an open man, you try to get the ball to him. Just as soon as you make your pass, you ought to be moving. The principle is known in basketball as the *pass and cut*. Hit the open man, pass to him, then try to get open again yourself by moving toward the areas on the court from which you're able to shoot most accurately.

At the other end of the pass, don't let the ball get out of your sight, watch it all the way into your hands, and catch it with relaxed fingers—sort of absorb the pass, don't fight it. The receiver also ought to be moving toward the pass, and, even before he has it safely, he ought to be calculating what he's going to do with the ball—shoot, drive, dribble, or pass—when he gets it. I'd say the one thing that's made me a good pro despite my lack of size is that I'm not only quick in my movements but also quick in my decisions.

A passer has to consider the man he's trying to reach. Some players have good hands and can handle a pass with plenty of zing behind it, while others have trouble holding on to a ball if it's thrown too hard. Some players can reach down for a pass if they have to, even if it's down around their knees. On all passes, nevertheless, I try to get the ball to the man chest-high, where it's easiest for most players to handle.

I've been asked over the years whether I have a special problem because I'm left-handed, because the spin and rotation on the ball would be opposite from what right-handed players are used to. Actually, there's no problem at all—or seldom any problem, anyway—because most of the passes I throw are in a forward direction, with the rotation in the direction of my target, the same as any other player's. The long, overhand baseball-style pass from one end of the floor to the other is a valuable weapon, although it can be tricky to throw, no matter which hand you use. I try to make my follow-through straight ahead and downward to avoid sideways rotation, which might make the ball curve, and I also try to make sure I don't throw too long. Bounce passes are another useful

Gail Goodrich has himself and the ball perfectly in control to pass, shoot, or drive toward the basket.

method of getting the ball to the open man, and on these passes, too, I take care to make the spin forward rather than in another direction, because a ball is apt to carom way off target, otherwise, after it hits the floor.

Passing to your pivot man takes in some other problems, because centers usually don't want the ball until they're in position to do something with it. There aren't many big men who dribble well— it's too long a bounce for them from their hands to the floor and back, and the ball can be stolen more easily if they try. Wilt Chamberlain and the other Lakers have learned each other's habits so that we can look at him and he looks back at us and we sort of eye signal each other when he's ready for the pass. The communication that Jerry West and I have developed with each other in the backcourt is even more subtle than an eye contact. We've played together enough to know each other's habits, to know what each of us is most likely to do in a situation, and we sort of instinctively, by now, work together to get each other the ball when either of us is open for a good shot. The kind of almost automatic way that Jerry and I work together is something players and teams have to develop the hard way—by playing together long enough so they know each other's favorite positions, favorite moves and styles so thoroughly, nobody even has to stop to think about them. That's what players mean when they refer to *learning each other's moves*, and unfortunately there doesn't seem to be any way to telescope the process. Teams that keep the same basic line-up for two or three straight seasons have a built-in edge over shuffled or new teams, no matter how much individual talent the latter may have. To get back to the point I was making about getting the ball to the pivot man, I like to use what—if you have to have a label—is called a two-handed overhead snap pass to get the ball in to Wilt, because it's quick and accurate and also because I can fake a drive or shot off the same motion.

Passing and moving quickly are at the heart of what may be the most basic two-man situation in the game, the *give-and-go*. The play can be used by any two players and any place on the floor, and it's simply a quick, short pass you throw, then you make your quick cut. The defensive player assigned to you is going to relax momentarily when you give up the ball, and, when he does, the man you've passed to zips it right back. You should be open for a shot or be able to drive in that instant of freedom you have before your defender recovers.

The wife of a friend of mine had trouble understanding the phrase. I guess she thought it was something like eating and running. He and I were talking basketball one night when she interrupted to snort indignantly: "I think it's rude to give and go!"

If "hot dog" is a label to be avoided, "playmaker" is one any basketball player wears with honor. To make a wild pass that flies out of bounds because its target could not handle it is a failure, but to pass to a man who then scores a basket is a fundamental objective of the game.

Playmakers are in short supply in pro basketball because so few bigger guards learn the techniques in their high-school and college days and because the little men who *do* learn them may become defensive liabilities at the professional level. Bob Cousy, an NBA coach now, but before that a star for the Boston Celtics for fourteen seasons, is the model for all playmakers, and among those who most cleverly have followed in his mold is Mahdi Abdul-Rahman (until 1972 he was Walt Hazzard) of the Golden State Warriors. His contribution to this book was written before October 1972 while he was playmaker for the Buffalo Braves. Still another ex-UCLA All-American, Abdul-Rahman is a good defensive player at 6-foot-3 but has made his greatest mark as a professional by being a resourceful floor leader and playmaker, virtually a coach on the floor.

Mahdi
Abdul-Rahman

There may be some players who are natural-born playmakers. I envy them. Playmaking is my job with Buffalo and has been my specialty through my entire pro career, but there was nothing natural for me in learning the trade.

By rights, I should be a shooting guard more than a passer, because that's how I started out on the schoolyards in Philadelphia, an area that has produced some of the best players in NBA history, including Wilt Chamberlain, Ray Scott, Guy Rodgers, and a guy who's done well in another field, Bill Cosby, to name a few. I followed Wilt by a few years at Overbrook High, and we had a great team, with Wayne Hightower playing up front, with me the shooter in the backcourt, and with Wali Jones—yes, the same Wali Jones who plays now for Milwaukee—our "quarterback."

It wasn't until my sophomore year in college, when I got to UCLA, that I was asked to switch from thinking first about my own scoring to thinking about rolling up *assists*, and I think that having to make the change that late in my basketball life forced me to make an analysis of what's involved. I also think that my ability to shoot the ball is a big factor in whatever success I have as a playmaker, because teams know they can't relax on me. If they give me room waiting for me to pass, I'll put the ball in the hole. Play me too tight to stop my shooting and my passing game opens up.

Creating a dilemma for the defense is what playmaking is all about, I believe. There's no situation when this is more true than on the fast break. Directing the fast break properly is probably the most important thing a playmaker does. The idea is to get a 3-on-2 or 2-on-1 or 4-on-3 situation, get an easy shot before the defense can get into position. It's the playmaker's job to make sure that, once you've gotten the overload situation, your team makes sure to exploit it.

The first thing that has to happen is that the fast break has to be run properly. The outlet pass from the defensive rebounder has to be a good one, and the playmaker has to try to take the middle of the floor down toward the hoop, so that you keep open the most possible choices of play. One guard ought to head down the right side of the floor and one of the forwards the left side, so that you're doing what's called *filling the lanes.* Men have to keep spread out, because if two offensive players head downcourt too close together, one defensive player can cover both of them at once and the overload situation is gone. As the playmaker reaches the free-throw circle, he has to weigh the situation and see where his men are, where the defenders are, using his peripheral (or sideways) vision. I try to dribble toward the closest defensive player. If he comes up to meet me, there's got to be one of my teammates open and I can bounce-pass to him for a layup. If the defensive players hang back to cut off my pass to one side or the other, I'm open for the jump or to continue my drive right to the hoop for a layup. The playmaker wants to stop at about the free-throw line, but he has to be careful neither to get too deep nor to stop his dribble too soon. Penetration is a goal.

On set plays and set patterns, your passes are predetermined. But most of the time pros are free-lancing, and here's where being a playmaker can get tricky. All your players want to get their shots, and they all want to handle the ball. Other things being equal, it's wise to try to make sure as a playmaker that all your guys get their share of shots. You never want to get in the habit of passing always to just one man, because he may love you like a brother and three other guys will want your head on a platter. When players sulk, they stop moving and the whole offense stagnates. If guys think they'll

Abdul-Rahman drives furiously toward the hoop, prepared to shoot or to pass off to an open man if defense slides over to stop him.

get the ball if they get open, they'll work harder at moving without the ball, and opportunities open up for everybody.

If all five men in an offense are doing their jobs properly, four men are working to get to places on the floor from which they're high-percentage shooters, and the fifth guy, the one with the ball, is looking for one of the four to shoot. A playmaker has to know his teammates well enough to know where each man's high-percentage area is. It doesn't do much good, for example, for me to pass to our big center, Elmore Smith, out around the top of the key. That's too far for him. We have some good outside-shooting *guards*, though, and they're the men for me to look for deep.

All the time I'm looking for my own shot too, because I know that, if I get too pass-conscious, the defense can play me entirely to pass, use my defender to sag back and double-team on Smith or elsewhere, and we're stopped cold.

You can see that being a playmaker really is a lot like being the leader of an orchestra. You have to keep balance all the time, not too much brass and not too much strings. Not too much outside shooting by the guard and not too many dunks by the center. It's a delicate job and a hard one, but I've learned to love it.

What offensive teams have to scheme and work to gain against most opponents—the mismatch—they get automatically when they confront the Houston Rockets and their explosive Calvin Murphy. But they do not automatically convert their apparent advantage into victories.

The gritty 5-foot-9, 165-pound former All-American from Niagara University is the smallest player to become a significant contributor to an NBA team in nearly two decades, delighting fans and his teammates alike with his clever passing and accurate shooting. He has made his mark primarily through his offensive play, but the special tactics he's developed for himself defensively are what have earned him the chance to prove his ability.

Calvin Murphy

Forgive me if I come on strong. It's just that I'm tired of justifying myself. I happen to think size is overrated, and I think I've proved it. I've proved, in fact, that I can get my shots off in the NBA, I've proved that I can play defense in the NBA, I've proved I can't be bullied. I had confidence in my game when no one else did. I never doubted my ability—even if other people used to.

My first time around the league in my rookie season (when the Rockets played in San Diego), every team we played against for the first time would try to force me to play against their biggest backcourt man and would try to force me to guard him close to the basket. From close range—in their theory anyway—the man could shoot over me with ease. That's what teams traditionally have done against small opponents; *taking a man into the hole,* or *taking him into the pivot,* it's called. They had to disrupt their entire normal offense, though, to do this, and they also took a lot of time by pro standards to set up their plan. After all that, they still didn't wind up with the bonanza they thought they would, it pleases me to point out.

The 24-second clock works in my favor, and so do the ideas we worked out on the Rockets so that I could more than hold my own defensively, then still be able to do the things I can which make me dangerous on offense. By the time teams maneuver me toward the pivot—I hold my ground, scramble, scratch, and do whatever I can to keep out of there—they use up 18 or 19 seconds, and then they have to rush a bad shot. That first year, before teams wised up, Elvin Hayes used to gobble up the defensive rebounds, and often we'd have good fast-break possibilities with him throwing the full-court pass to a guard or to our forwards after a miss. Elvin also helped me another way because he's such a great shot-blocker and so quick. I could—and still do—play up tight on my man, protecting more against the outside shot than against the drive, because I know that if my man gets loose and goes around me to drive for a layup, chances are my center can pick the man up and block him.

Trying to exploit me, teams usually fouled up their offense more than they helped it. They stopped doing what they do best and went to unfamiliar things. If they tried to muscle me around, I'd just muscle back. The respect of your opponents is a big thing in the pros. When I come into a game and the other team's superstar is playing me, then I know that I've earned that team's respect. At the start of my rookie year, when we played Los Angeles, Jerry West didn't guard me. But at the end of the season they had West checking me. That meant something to me.

I've played basketball most of my life, starting when I was a kid in Norwalk, Connecticut, and would find a way every summer during my high-school days to go to the camp that Red Auerbach used to run in Massachusetts. They tell me that when he was coach of the Celtics he'd travel from city to city with the team and, when he was asked questions about the Celtics he didn't want to answer, he'd dodge the issue by telling reporters about this great little kid from Connecticut who was going to be such a great college star someday. Looking back, I guess I *was* a little unusual—but I didn't dare let myself think that way. I taught myself to dribble equally well with both hands, taught myself to dribble with good control and make my moves without ever having to look down at the ball (a *must* for any decent ball-handler), taught myself to make quick, accurate passes and to shoot accurately and quickly from awkward —awkward for other people, that is—positions. I also could dunk, which I don't do much in NBA games—but the jumping ability that dunking requires helps me all over the court.

If I permit a man to take me deep, sure he's got an edge. So I try to avoid that by picking him up early—maybe even before he crosses the halfcourt line. I scramble and work at him, trying not to give him an inch, trying to keep the ball from him or trying to make him pass it off before he gets into danger areas. I think I have one advantage over the big guards—they have to dribble high, and I can move in and steal the ball. It's something they have no way to do to me.

Another trick that teams try against me—and teams try generally to create mismatches—is to try to run me into picks. What they want is for me to make a defensive switch so that I'll be guarding that team's center or a forward instead of their guard. They'd love to work the old *pick and roll* play on me by having the center head for the basket after the switch, take a lob pass over my head, and then dunk it. This is a play most teams have in their offenses, trying in general to get a guard defending against a center. The antidote is to slide or fight past the pick in the first place.

I probably burn more energy than most other players in the league playing defense, but don't forget I'm doing some things—using my quickness and my speed—when *I* have the ball, and by the fourth period the guy who's been guarding me often is lots more bushed, more disorganized trying to shut me off, than I am playing against him. A pro basketball player's life is a good one, and I'm willing to work as hard as I have to, to keep enjoying it. Coming out of college I wasn't drafted until the second round, and everybody told me that a little man just can't make it in the NBA. I've got the last laugh, though, and excuse me if it's a loud one.

Opportunities are wasted in the NBA unless a team is prepared to act and react quickly. The Boston Celtics, having gone through a difficult rebuilding period following the retirement of such all-time greats as Bill Russell, K. C. Jones, Sam Jones, and others, once again are consistent winners, and a key to their comeback has been the ability to make the right move at the right time. The process is both mental and physical, in ways which former Kansas All-American Jo Jo White has had to master. The 6-foot-3, 190-pound former U.S. Olympic Games performer is the Celtics' on-court leader.

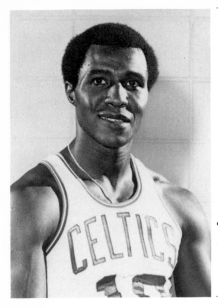

Jo Jo White

I'm asked to talk to service clubs and youth groups in and around Boston all the time, and when I accept those invitations and explain about how the Celtics feel we have to play a running game in order to win, fans seem surprised to learn that so much of what pro basketball teams do is improvised and spur-of-the-moment rather than prearranged. They know that basketball teams have what are called "plays," and people know that plays are vital in football, so they expect basketball teams to rely on planned things in the same way.

The truth is that, because of the abilities of pro defenses and because of the 24-second clock's pressure on a team to shoot in a hurry, set plays are things you resort to only when you're not running and only when you need to exploit a special situation. Set plays and patterns give teams a way to get something done quickly —while the situation still exists—without having to waste a time out to discuss things, without giving your opponent time to re-adjust.

We're playing Detroit, say, and our center, Dave Cowens, has been giving the Pistons' pivot man, Bob Lanier, fits. Let's say that Lanier picks up his fourth foul. Naturally we want to exploit that

by having Dave drive on Lanier, force him either to concede Dave
the shot or pick up still another foul if he tries to guard him close.
An easy way to do it is for me, as the playmaker, to bring the ball
up and call one of our plays that call for Dave to have the ball.
By calling a play, I'm making sure all five of our guys know immediately what we're trying to do, and they all have assignments to
carry out. If it's Curtis Rowe or one of the Detroit forwards who
gets into foul trouble, I can call a play for John Havlicek or one
of our other forwards. If Detroit substitutes for the man in foul
trouble and sends a player into the game I think we can exploit,
we can go to a play that will do it. The only other way to get
something done in a planned, organized way is to call for a time
out.

The plays themselves are no big thing. They're simple, like most
pro teams' plays—a single pass and cut, a crisscross to force a switch
that gives us a mismatch—simple things that don't take much time
to set up and don't require absolutely perfect timing. We're not
fooling the other team—they probably know our plays as well as we
do, just as we know their plays after facing them a few times in the
season. Even if they know we're going to work on Lanier, they
still have to make an adjustment, and when they do adjust, we'll
hope to get enough of an edge to put some points up on the scoreboard.

The Celtics have only about eight plays, with three or four
options on each one. There's a play for each of our five positions,
plus plays we may change around a little from year to year if we
have a player who's especially dangerous from a particular spot.
Always we're trying to get the fast break, get down the floor in a
hurry. When we don't get the break, or when we bring the ball
down the floor from out of bounds after the other team has scored,
we'll usually try a play so we'll either be working on a weak defensive man or somebody in foul trouble, or, if nothing else, so
we'll all be moving into something coordinated. Without a play
it's an easy thing to start standing around, to loaf. Besides, plays
or patterns, if carried out like they're designed, leave teams in good
rebounding and defensive positions.

If the plays aren't fancy, neither is the way we call them. Usually
you'll use your voice and the hand you're not using to dribble the
ball. "Two!" I might yell, and I'll raise my hand with a "V for
Victory," two fingers up, repeating it and turning so I'm sure

everyone sees me and is aware of the play, and at the same time continuing on up the floor. Most teams have some bread-and-butter basic play they call "the fist" because it's so easy to recognize from all over the floor. Voice and hand signals are both used, because you want to communicate over the noise of the crowd. Some teams don't use numbers for their plays, but some nickname or a letter of the alphabet or the name of a city or some combination of all of them. If the Knicks work a cute play for a forward and some other team decides to copy it, they might call it "New York," even if the Knicks call it "Three." If you use an option off one of your plays—maybe the forward is supposed to stop for an outside jump shot instead of penetrating for a layup—you might call, "Two-C!" or "A-One!"

The playmaker of a team is the guy who yells the play and who's responsible for making sure everybody knows it, but the selection of what play to call might be his or the coach's, depending on him, on the coach, and on the game situation. Some coaches call all the plays; some leave it up to the players—and, at that, only when you need them, usually. Coming back onto the floor after a time out, teams often will get a play from the coach and no one needs to yell it because it's the last thing he says before sending his men back onto the floor.

A coach may use color codes for his defenses, something as simple as "green" when he wants his team to gamble, press, scramble, not worry about fouling, and "red" when he wants to avoid fouls, play more conservatively. He's not fooling the other team—they know what kind of defense is going to be played just as soon as his team does. By yelling just that one word, and maybe screaming it an extra time or two, he's sure of getting the message to all five of his players at once without having to use up a time out.

Even though plays are simple, there's usually one guy on every team who has trouble remembering them. The play will call for him to set a screen on the left of the key, and he'll wind up at the top of the circle, waiting to get the ball so he can pass to a cutter who never shows up. Some guys in the league are notorious about forgetting plays, and they get needled not only by their teammates but also by the other teams' players.

Pros may forget the plays for every man on their team, but—funny thing—they never seem to have trouble remembering the plays that give them the shots. We're beautiful people, we are, basketball pros. We play a team sport, but the team part gets kind of blurred sometimes.

That action continues at rapid pace is one of the attractions of pro basketball for many of its followers. When two fast-breaking teams are playing, they sprint back and forth almost as quickly, it seems, as a tennis ball volleys between two men at the net. There are some respites, however, and these moments provide opportunity for the fan to sit back and savor what he's just seen.

Jump-ball and out-of-bounds situations are two of these temporary moments of lull, and while spectators calm their breathing, players tense for moments of sudden fury within the general flow of an already furious sport.

Spencer Haywood of the Seattle Supersonics is familiar with crisis, for he led the United States to the 1968 Olympic Games championship, earned Most Valuable Player and Rookie of the Year honors in the American Basketball Association, and then joined the NBA in 1971, following a landmark federal court decision that changed the pattern of pro sports' traditional rookie draft systems. Compared to the legal ruling that opened the way for undergraduate collegians to become pros under controlled, regulated circumstances, jump balls and out-of-bounds plays are inconsequential. In winning and losing basketball games, however, they often prove vital.

Spencer Haywood

There's something special about the opening tip-off, a build-up of pressure and tension and excitement and nerves that chokes at you until you just about want to scream. Then the referee tosses the ball high up in the air between you and the jumper for the other team, you reach way up after it in an explosion of energy you've been building up to all day—and all of a sudden things are in place again, the way you're used to them. The pressure's off, and you can just start playing your game.

Leading up to the Olympics, to my first pro game, and to my first game in the NBA, I was so edgy that if somebody had tapped me on the shoulder, I think I'd have broken every high-jumping record ever set. Once the tips happened, I was Mr. Ice Water again and relaxed into the rhythm of the game.

I play forward for the Supersonics, but I've played mostly center before in my career, and I'm still in on the opening tip-offs most of the time. Every quarter of a game opens with a jump ball between the opposing centers (or best jumpers, in my case), and a team that can control all four and also get baskets every time earns a pretty good bulge on the way to a win. The play takes maybe two or three seconds—but two seconds is enough to clinch a win or blow a game.

Jumping ability isn't the whole story. If the Sonics are to get possession, somebody on my team is going to have to make sure to grab the ball if I tip it to him, and then our other players have to be alert to move toward our basket quickly for our shot. I was taught a long time ago to go up one-handed, which gives me the fullest possible extension of my body, and to try to tip the ball with a flick of my wrist rather than slap at it. I like to think positively about getting tips, but I suppose I also have to point out that if we lose the tip we've got to be just as alert to go to our defense and to try to steal the ball ourselves.

All sorts of psyching is happening when there's a jump ball coming up, and I doubt that many fans realize all the strategy that goes on. The two jumpers will sometimes growl at each other or taunt each other, try to stare each other down like a couple of boxers getting their instructions in the middle of the ring before a championship fight. Some guys are chatty and want to talk; others pretend you're not even there. Definite plays are set up, calling for the jumper to try to control the direction of the ball— not just slam it wildly—and for the other men to cut toward the basket for a pass and quick shot. It's aggravating that referees are inconsistent in the way they toss the ball—no two guys throw it up the same height, and some don't get it going straight up at all. Since I do so much center jumping, I try to study each referee's habits and make mental notes. I try to time my jump to be up there at the full height of the toss so I can get the ball, and I'm alert for refs who consistently throw at an angle. I figure I've got about an even chance or a better than even chance against most of the guys I go up against, so I like to stay a bit away from the line, give myself some room. Against the giants like Kareem Jabbar, Wilt Chamberlain, and Nate Thurmond, I try to psych them by crowding them a little, getting as close as I can to the line without getting in danger of crossing over or of fouling by hitting the man on the way up. Your team loses the ball if you tip the ball while it's still on its way up, so you try to make sure of your timing— even though guys will try to sneak a quick tap and sometimes get away with it.

Jump balls are also called when a defensive man ties up an

offensive player by grabbing the ball, when the ball goes out of bounds and was touched simultaneously by an offensive and defensive man, and when you make a clean block on a ball and force the shooter to come down with it still in his hands. Teams judge who the two jumpers are, sometimes about equal in size or jumping ability, but sometimes a guard has to jump against the other team's center. You set up accordingly, prepared with an offensive play to take advantage of getting possession or with a defensive play if you figure you'll probably lose the tip. Teams have to be realistic —you can't root for your man just because he's wearing the same color shirt you are. You have to make a decision and follow through on it.

Out-of-bounds plays are another way to get a couple of points here, a couple of points there, which you otherwise might not get. Teams drill hard at getting timing and passing right on these plays. The key out-of-bounds situations are the ones behind your own basket, and coaches design plays usually so there's a man inside who'll get the ball if he's open and another man way deep, toward midcourt as a "safety valve" so you'll be sure to get the ball into play within the required 5 seconds. The referee who calls the out-of-bounds designates the player who makes the in-bounds pass, and the coach or that player will yell and signal for the play. If I'm the biggest man on the floor for the Sonics and have to take the ball out, we'll use a play setting up more of an outside shot than a try for a play on the boards because, as you can see, there's no point to trying something that probably isn't going to succeed. Defenses will either crowd the in-bounds man and block his passing angles, or sometimes drop back to prevent him from having a clear target. Possession of the ball is so important that guys usually will call time out rather than risk turning the ball back over because they can't get it in play in time. Most teams have four or five different plays to use, and they start with a voice signal and usually by the in-bounding man's slapping the ball hard.

The NBA rule in the last 3 minutes of a game is that, after the other team scores, you can put the ball in play from midcourt instead of from underneath their basket, so you can save 47 feet of work and the time it would take to dribble that far by calling time out as soon as the ball falls through the net. Often we'll alert the ref that we're going to call time, and that way we save even a little bit more time because he's ready to call it. You have your choice of which side of the floor you pass in from, and every team has a special play or two it saves for a last possible winning or tying shot attempt, even if there's only one or two seconds left on the clock. It seems that every season five or six games are won because a team is able to make this play work. When you're on the nervous end of that situation, trying to protect a lead, you'll usually double-team and overplay the one or two men on the other team you figure will try the shot—Jabbar or Oscar Robertson if you're play-ing Milwaukee, Dave Bing or big Bob Lanier if you're playing Detroit, Willis Reed or Earl Monroe or Walt Frazier if you're play-ing New York, Jeff Mullins or Rick Barry if you're playing Golden State, and so on down the list.

It's really rough on a new player until he's been around the league a few times and learns which players are the quick shooters, which guys are the leapers, which guys are the ball-handlers, and which guys are the crashers. My biggest difficulty coming into the NBA in the unusual way I did wasn't physical. I knew what things I could do, and I didn't lack confidence in myself. But I had to cram my learning time into practically no time at all in those first few games I played for the Sonics, and looking back I'm sorry —but not surprised—that I may have disappointed some people by not being more spectacular right off the bat. I proved the hard way that a guy needs to be mentally ready and has to have plenty of savvy to succeed in the NBA. Raw talent isn't enough. I like to think I've made my contribution toward making Seattle a con-tender, but, boy, that early going was a nightmare.

7

MOMENTUM IS THE
NAME OF THE GAME

Fred Schaus is a burly 6-foot-6 son of the East Ohio and West Virginia hill country who rose at dawn several times a week to play a fast set of tennis, keep his weight in reasonable check, and still be at his desk in the catacombs of the Forum in Inglewood, California, in time to take up the responsibilities of being one of the NBA's most astute general managers. Before he filled an executive's role with the Los Angeles Lakers, he was the team's coach for its first seven years in Los Angeles and he is regarded as one of the best thinkers in the game—now as coach at Purdue following his resignation from the Laker organization after the Lakers won the 1971–72 NBA title.

An ex-Laker sought him out one day for advice. He was embarking on a coaching career of his own at the high-school level and hoped to gain some special insight, some special secret which might make his teams' records as flossy as Schaus's.

The big man, a former West Virginia University star, a former standout player in the NBA's early years, a successful collegiate coach back at WVU (among his products: Hot Rod Hundley, Jerry West, and Rod Thorn), and then pro coach, considered the question with characteristic deliberation.

"The best advice I can give you," Schaus drawled with exaggeratedly apparent wisdom as the ex-player pulled out a notepad and pencil and began writing, "is to get an early lead—and then increase it!"

And then Schaus grinned a sardonic grin, shared a chuckle with the momentarily dumfounded information-seeker, and finally diagramed a few pet out-of-bounds plays and defenses which he felt would be more helpful than the joke.

The verbal hotfoot contained, as wit often does, a germ of truth. The ebb-and-flow in basketball is constant, and teams able to jump ahead early in a game do indeed have advantage because they are able to play more loosely, are able to control the pace, and, to a degree, are able to dictate tactics. Circumstances change rapidly, however, and it usually falls to a team's coach and its playmaker to provide the appropriate direction at the appropriate time.

Pete Maravich of the Atlanta Hawks, one of the most publicized collegians ever to enter the NBA following an NCAA record-setting scoring career as All-American at Louisiana State University, is more aware of game dynamics than some pros because he is the son of an outstanding collegiate coach, Press Maravich, and has been on game sidelines and in the workout gyms all his life. Renowned for his shaggy hair and floppy socks, for his little-boy-lost look, the 6-foot-5 200-pounder has earned wide respect for his basketball thinking, as well as for his spectacular style of play.

Pete Maravich

Momentum is lots easier for me to feel in a game than to describe in print. When you've got it—when you're racing up and down the floor, sinking everything your team throws up at your end and choking off the offense at the other, when you roll up five, six, seven baskets in a row and can't seem to do anything wrong—that's beautiful, man, just simply beautiful. All five of your guys are contributing together, working in a unit. It's not five guys, really, when you get a truly hot streak going. It's like you're all part of a single mind and body, like you're all in each others' heads and all feeling and seeing and reacting exactly the same way. You feel like it'll go on forever, like it'll never stop. You feel like you're 20 feet tall.

Winning in pro ball demands that your team generate a hot streak at some point in the game but, more than that, that it generate at least two. I can't explain why this is, but I do know that, when you look back over a season, you see that in most games there was one spurt by either team and that the winning club was the one that could generate a second.

Every game you play is a little bit different from every other game, but, it seems to me, often they start out something like the first round of a boxing match. Boxers try the jab and then the hook. And in basketball the Hawks might work a play for Lou Hudson early, then one for me, then one for our center. We're looking to get something going, and maybe we'll score, they'll score, we'll score, they'll score, and then—suddenly—something explodes. A sort of sixth sense tells you it's building. A fast break or a steal often will be the ignition, and in a few seconds a close game is turning into a rout before the momentum stops cold—just as suddenly as it began. A great defensive play can cool off a hot team, or a charging foul on one of its guys or maybe a questionable call by one of the refs.

I don't like to wait for momentum to generate itself. Ever since high school, I've found that I can sometimes get my team hot with a behind-the-back pass or a razzle-dazzle drive—one of the plays that people sometimes call me a "hot dog" for trying. I explain that I'm making those plays with a purpose, not just showboating, but some guys are hard to convince. I've had it happen often enough to know I'm right—for me. I make plays I know I can make because I've practiced them and practiced them. I might look bad if a play I try fizzles, but that's part of the game too. You take the calculated risk.

What happens more often than not in an NBA game is that after you generate a spurt and build up a comfortable lead, you'll sort of take stock of things and consider what's happened. After a spurt cools off, there's time to think about what guys on the other team are in foul trouble or seem to be having bad nights, and you can size up your own players too. That's part of my job on the Hawks, with advice and suggestions from the coach. Teams seem to go back into what we call a *trading* situation—that you-score-we-score-you-score thing. The team that trails will try anything it can to get momentum and get back into a game, and the team that's ahead tries to avoid turnovers, tries to get at least a good-percentage shot every time it comes down the floor, plays the tough defense, tries to keep about the same difference in the point spread there was when the streak cooled off. Coaches on the trailing team will make substitutions a lot more frequently in these moments, trying to find a hot shooter or somebody who can wake things up. As the team that's leading, you try to avoid mistakes and also make sure to play tough defense on the new man. Everybody in the NBA is a good shooter, but some guys seem to be hit-or-miss unless they click on their first two or three tries in a game. There are plenty of guys coming off the bench who will kill you if they get a few quick hoops, get their confidence going—and their personal momentum can spread to the other four players unless you discourage them early. Tough defense early in a game is important so none of the starters get red hot—if you can help it.

If playing on a team generating momentum is a tremendous lift for you emotionally, playing on a team that's in the middle of being blitzed is sheer hell. Coaches have to be even more alert than the players, I think, to the momentum going one way or the other —because they've got perspective as nonparticipants, and they try to cool the team they're playing against by calling a time out. That's the first, best weapon teams have to stop the other club's momentum. If you watch a few games, I'm sure you'll see this happen frequently. You try anything you can to break their mental concentration, break their rhythm.

A coach has to be careful, though, because he gets only seven time outs in a game, no more than four in the last period, and he almost automatically has four used up which he doesn't have much control over. Let's face it. Radio and television income is vital to every team in the NBA, and years ago the league recognized the facts of life by putting in a rule to insure that there are at least two time outs every period. Stations could be sure to get in their commercials that way. The rule reads that unless a time out has been called earlier for tactical reasons by one team or the other, the home team has to call time out between the $7\frac{1}{2}$- and 6-minutes-to-go marks of every quarter. Unless there's been a second one before then, the visiting coach is supposed to call *his* time out between the $3\frac{1}{2}$- and 2-minute marks. The time outs are kept track of at the scorers' table, and the referee will tell the coaches when their time is due.

Balancing those mandatory time outs against the time outs you have to hoard to stop the other team's momentum or introduce a new strategy or simply give your team a rest is so delicate a job that coaches take that responsibility themselves. Any player on the floor is eligible to call the time out, but nobody had better do it unless the coach yells for one first.

Don't think that finesse on time outs stops at the players' benches, either. The radio-TV stations that broadcast NBA games sell commercials on the basis of two per quarter of play—not to mention all the plugs they care to sell before the game, during halftime, and afterward. There's one announcer in the league who makes himself and his sponsors out to be big heroes. The game he's calling may get red hot in the final quarter—one team up by only a couple of points—and it's after there've already been two time outs. If one of the teams calls a real, *actually needed* time out for a win-or-lose reason, the sportscaster will get his voice all excited and scream at his listeners, "Our sponsors have told me, at a crucial time like this, forget about the commercials! Forget about our message! Just talk about the game!"

No matter how large his bonuses, no matter how large his annual salary, no professional athlete tolerates easily the stigma of being a reserve. With rare exceptions, he's usually been the star player—the center of attention—every place he's played prior to reaching the ultimate plateau, and it eats at a man who's used to adulation to sit on a bench while five other men perform. A man satisfied with inactivity probably lacks sufficient competitive instinct to have earned a roster spot in the first place, in fact.

Cazzie Russell of the Golden State Warriors has known the bitterness of being a reserve, although he has come now to be one of the NBA's leading performers as a starter. Three-time All-American at the University of Michigan and before that heralded as the finest high-school basketball player in the history of the city of Chicago, the 6-foot-5½, 220-pound Russell was number-one draft choice of the New York Knicks in 1966 and for a while was a starter. A broken ankle in January of 1970 kept him idled until the playoffs and elevated Bill Bradley to a starting job he has held ever since. The following season Russell was that difficult-to-accept thing, the "sixth man," before being traded to the Warriors in the spring of 1971 in a transaction that sent Jerry Lucas to New York in exchange.

The emotional ups and downs were not easy for Russell to accept, for he is a proud and vigorous man. Assured now of a star regular's recognition, he also knows what it is to be a substitute.

Cazzie Russell

The writers, the front-office people, your pals, kids asking for your autograph—you get it from all of them. "Keep up the good work, Caz. Way to hang in there, Caz. Way to come off the bench firing. Way to go . . ."

Pregame tension isn't any less for a nonstarter than it is for the regulars, only they get to burn it off immediately after the tip-off because they're in the game. The "sixth man" or "seventh man" goes through the same pregame process of warm-up and psyching himself—and then puts his sweats back on to sit on the bench. If the five starters go well, if your team takes command, you might sit there for 20 minutes before the coach calls you, and by then you're cooled off, stiff, without that surge of energy you had when the game started. Maybe you never get called at all.

I'd listen to it all the time—that I'd be starting on any other ball club except the Knicks, that I could make the all-star team. I chafed and growled at being on the bench, yet I couldn't get angry at Coach Holzman or at Bill Bradley or at anybody else because the Knicks were winners, and no coach breaks up a winning combination. Bench guys on losing teams have it tougher because they feel that if they were playing more they could turn things around.

Being traded to the Warriors was a happy thing for me, even though I'd made lots of friends in New York. I've come to enjoy the Bay Area and the West Coast, and it was a thrill to make the all-star game for the first time in January of '72. It was acknowledgment of the consistency of my effort, proof that hard work still pays off.

The horrible thing about being a reserve, for most players, is that it's so tough to keep in top physical condition once the regular season begins. With eighty-two games to be squeezed into the schedule between October and March, teams are either traveling between cities or playing just about every night. Coaches squeeze in what workouts they can, but even then they have to spend most of their time working with their regulars. The reserves don't get the game-playing time they need to stay in top shape, yet there's not enough workout time to keep fit, either. Unless a guy takes it as his own responsibility, that is—which is the decision I made, and which, I think, made possible the success I've had.

Knowing it was pretty much up to me what kind of shape I'd be in—knowing that Coach Holzman had worked all of us hard in preseason camp but that it's easy to lose that peak if you don't keep working—I made it a point to really pour it on during the practices we'd have, and I'd come out early before games to shoot and run. There'd be a few ushers, some venders, the Western Union operator, and me all alone out in the Garden—but I knew what I was after. Players have joked at me for years about my eating habits, and I'm used to the kidding by now. I'm convinced that eating the right foods, supplementing my diet with additional vitamins and minerals and proteins, is very important to me—makes me stronger, gives me more endurance, helps me fight off colds. Even now, as a starter with the Warriors, I do extra work. We practice—when we can—at San Bruno Rec Center, down the peninsula from San Francisco, and I'll frequently go to a health spa after a workout and take a steam bath. Then I'll go home—I'm a bachelor—and have a light meal. I might do some reading, take a nap afterward. Around seven o'clock I go down to the gym at San Mateo High School and work on my game at night—just running and shooting and free throws. I get in fourteen or fifteen extra workouts a month that way, and I know that they've helped me a lot. I also do extra

calisthenics, even when we're on the road. If I were still coming
off the bench rather than a starter, all this extra work and care
would help me all that much more.

Playing in high school and college, where you're usually the star
of the team, you're taught to pace yourself, loaf at times—unlike
pro ball, players are encouraged by some coaches to loaf on defense
instead of offense—and you learn to save something to start or to
douse a final last-minute rally. NBA superstars keep those habits,
except that, as I've said, any loafing they do in a game is likely to
be on offense.

Coming off the bench is something else altogether, something to
which some men never adjust. Instead of pacing themselves as
they're used to doing, reserves must go into a game when they're
called and go at full speed, work as hard as they can. Most coaches
want 100 per cent effort from subs, and when the man is exhausted,
they can bring him back to the bench. It's "exploding" instead of
warming up and getting into the rhythm of the game slowly, the
way a starter can. Players who can come off the bench and make
a change in the pattern of a game are worth gold to their club.
When I was a boy, I remember watching the Game of the Week on
TV and seeing Frank Ramsey come off the bench that way for
the Boston Celtics. John Havlicek was the best sixth man in basketball for half a dozen seasons with the Celts before he became a
starter, and Joe Ellis on the Warriors now is a great reserve. A big
plus for all three of these guys is that they could play either guard
or forward, but position doesn't seem to matter as much as being
able to get into absolutely top gear in a hurry.

Sitting on the bench, you must make extra effort to stay alert,
keep up with the game. I always tried to be on the watch for
situations when I might be called and to anticipate when I'd get
going. I'd study the man whom I'd probably have to defend so that
I wouldn't be a liability to my club even for a minute when I
started to play. You sort of try to keep up mentally with the tempo
of the game, then force your body to get up to that tempo once
you shed your sweats, report to the official scorer, and go in. Sometimes
the coach will tell you specifically what he wants you to do, but more
often he'll just holler for you. My game is shooting—getting points in
a hurry—and I just assumed that if the coach wanted me, that's what
he wanted me to do. In Ellis's case for our club, he doesn't need too
much specific instruction, either. If the Warriors go stale, can't

seem to generate anything, he goes in to get a rally started. If some player on the other club has been killing us, Joe's job would be to play super-tough defense on him. Subs on the bench with every team know by the second month of the season what kind of functions they're supposed to fill, and it's up to them to keep themselves fit to perform them.

Coaches really burn at the bench guys who complain, behind their backs or to them directly, that they're not playing enough. They also burn at the players who don't keep themselves ready. They *want* guys to stay eager, but they don't want troublemakers. Any player wants to contribute, wants to start. You don't like to be called "sixth man," even if people call you that as a compliment. The best policy is to mumble and grumble all the way to the bank.

In his rookie year with the New York Knicks—which marked his second year out of college, because he'd been cut in his first attempt at earning an NBA job—Mike Riordan seldom needed specific instructions from Coach Red Holzman when he was called off the bench to enter a game. Riordan was the ultimate pro basketball specialist—the man Holzman called upon to perform that whimsical aspect of pro basketball strategy which was known variously as the semi-intentional foul, giving a foul, taking a foul, or simply *giving one.*

Riordan became something of a national legend because of the way he was employed by the Knicks, but the 6-foot-4, 200-pound Providence College graduate did his job patiently, kept himself useful, and showed enough development by the following season to become a valued pro for deeper reasons. A trade in the fall of 1971 sent him to the Baltimore Bullets, for whom he became a valued all-around performer.

Riordan's ability to *give one* is no longer part of the game because of a rules change introduced in the fall of 1972, after he had already made his contribution to this book. Now when a player is fouled in what used to be a one-shot situation, his team gets the ball out of bounds. Thus there no longer is a tactical reason to commit that type of foul intentionally. As before, the fifth team foul of a period establishes a bonus shot, or *penalty shot,* on every subsequent foul. Riordan's comments are still entertaining, however, as this-is-how-it-used-to-be information.

Mike Riordan

I played an official 397 minutes in the 1968–69 season with the New York Knicks (out of a possible 3936 or so, 82 games times 48 minutes each) and was charged with 93 personal fouls. That averaged out, I figured out once the next year on a flight from New York to L.A., to about 1 foul every 4 minutes. I checked Wilt Chamberlain's stats for the same year, just for the heck of it, picking him to check up because he's so well known for never having fouled out of a game. While I was doing my 1-foul-every-4-minutes bit for my club, Wilt was committing a total of just 142 personals in 3669 minutes for the Lakers—about 1 every 32 minutes or so. I had to laugh at the difference.

Wilt doesn't *give* many fouls for his team, but that was just about my only duty with the Knicks in 1968–69, except for some playing time now and then with the other rinky-dinks off both benches when a game was already won or lost with just a few minutes left—what pros call *garbage time*. It would have been easy, I guess, for me to have gotten disgusted with just going into a game for 10 or 20 seconds at a time, but I had three years of college ball invested in my ambition to play in the NBA, and I'd sweated it out a season in the Eastern League after the Knicks cut me my first try at making the team. I'd been a twelfth-round draft choice in May of 1967, and even if I wasn't playing much as an NBA rookie, I at least had the satisfaction of knowing I was one of the few guys ever drafted that low who actually made the league. On official stats forms, you can't get less than 1 minute official credit even though you play less than that any time you enter a game; that's why I made the distinction about an *official* 397 minutes. I actually didn't even see *that* much action!

The NBA rules on personals separate *offensive fouls*, like charging or setting an illegal pick, from *defensive fouls*, such as blocking, hacking, and so forth. There are also what are called *loose-ball fouls*, and these generally are rebounding collisions when neither team has possession of the ball. Defensive and loose-ball fouls count against the individual, and they also count against the team. Starting with the fifth team foul of a period, with an exception I'll mention shortly, you go into the *bonus situation,* so that every team foul your side commits after that gives the guy who was fouled an extra free-throw attempt. If he is fouled in the act of shooting and misses the shot, he gets *three-to-make-two*; if he makes the shot even though he was fouled, he gets *two-to-make-one.* A foul committed on a man who isn't shooting gives the guy *one-plus-one*, or one free throw plus a bonus free throw, which he gets to attempt even if (unlike the college one-plus-one rule) he misses his first try. The bonus situation also goes into effect on the second foul of a period's last two minutes if the team isn't over the limit before that time.

I know this all can be very confusing to spectators who haven't seen too many pro games, but it's something you learn to take for granted with just a little experience watching NBA ball. It works more easily than it sounds, I mean.

Since possession of the ball has been figured by every coach to be worth darn near 2 points, the strategy was figured out long ago that, if your club wasn't in the bonus situation yet, and if the 2-minute mark hadn't come yet, it was good percentage to commit an intentional one-shot foul on the other team, giving up 1 point (or nothing at all if the free throw is missed) in order to get possession of the ball for a try at 2 or 3 points yourself. Games can even be clinched that way in the closing seconds. If you're 2 points ahead with practically no time left, the other team in possession of the ball, but with your club not in the bonus situation, a great strategy is to commit the one-shot foul, give the other team the point, get back the ball, and just kill the clock. There are other variations on this strategy, and the coaches have them all figured out, believe me.

Coach Holzman is one of a large group who feel that any little edge a team can earn is valuable, and he uses the *giving-a-foul* strategy just about whenever he can—even when the Knicks have a comfortable lead at the close of the first, second, or third period; you never can tell when the other club will spurt, catch up to you, and maybe gain the lead. A point edge early in a game may seem trivial in the first half, but look like 50 points late in the final quarter. At the same time, with the aggressive defense he had the Knicks playing anyway, Coach Holzman didn't want to risk getting his starting guards in danger of fouling out. That's where I came in. I was sort of a kamikaze man. I'd go into a game, commit a one-shot foul, and usually come right out again. The fans in New York are very, very hip on the inside things of basketball, and they'd cheer me as much for doing that little job, it seemed, as they would Dick Barnett when he made a great "fall back, baby" jump shot.

Less sophisticated fans may have thought of me as a hatchet man, but they were wrong. Even in as simple a thing as I was doing, I had to use some strategy and finesse.

For instance, teams would know why I was in the game and would be looking for me to commit the foul. Coming across the halfcourt line, for example, they'd force me to commit the foul in the last 2 minutes by delaying on their side of the line just long enough for the 2-minute mark to pass, but not so long that they'd be called for violating the 10-second rule. This cat-and-mouse game-within-a-game is why you'll often see an Oscar Robertson or an Earl Monroe or an Archie Clark or—hey, now that I'm a regular player—a Mike Riordan stalling briefly on one side of the halfcourt line while a defensive player stands in wait for him on the other.

Another finesse aspect of giving the foul is that you have to be quick, decisive, yet not *too* physical. If you give the man you're about to foul too much time, he'll get a wild shot of some kind going up and, instead of a one-shotter, he gets two free throws, defeating the strategy altogether, even though he didn't have a prayer that his shot would be good. You have to grab the man, maybe even wrap your arms completely around him, because if you just brush him or slap him, the referee might not call the foul at all. Referees have latitude in the rules to judge that a *flagrant* foul has been committed if a man gets too rough, and the penalty is two shots. Getting the refs to call the semi-intentional isn't always as simple as it ought to be, and sometimes you do it once, don't get the whistle, do it again, still don't get the whistle, hit the man a little harder next time—and find he's lost his temper and is taking a punch at you. What fights there are in the NBA seem often to start that way, because the ref doesn't call the first contact, and all you're trying to do is get a 1-point edge in a game.

Where the Knicks' strategy of using a man off the bench to give a foul is used, there's no need for a coach to have a special signal when he wants the foul to be given. Clubs that use their regular players to give the foul will have some word signal a coach can yell, and whichever player is not in foul trouble, near the dribbler, will do it. The code word might be a color or a nonsense word or the name of the team, "Royals!" or "Bullets!" or whatever. Everybody on both clubs knows when the play is coming, so deception really isn't important. Some teams just yell, "Give!" and have guys sitting on the bench yell it too. The idea is to make sure the refs know what's about to happen so they call the foul in a hurry. Some refs get so psyched occasionally they even call the foul before it actually takes place. You reach out for the dribbler, hear the whistle blowing, then make contact. It hasn't any bad effect on the game that way—but it sure could if the whistle was late. Other teams go to a particularly gambling defense, figuring they may get a steal and that the worst that can happen is the one-shot foul.

My second season with the Knicks, Howie Komives was traded to Detroit along with Walt Bellamy in the deal that brought us Dave DeBusschere, and Coach Holzman gave me the chance to prove I can do more in basketball than just give fouls. My playing time went from 397 minutes to 1677 as I replaced Howie as our "third guard," and my fouls went from 93 to 192, an "average" kind of NBA frequency of about 1 every 9 minutes for the aggressive defense I play. Johnny Warren, a rookie guard from St. John's, took over my special off-the-bench job in the great 1969–70 season when the Knicks won the world championship, and he gutted it out too—making his contribution in the same way I'd tried to, watching carefully from the bench and learning through observation. The next season he got a full-time chance with the new Cleveland team.

Maybe neither John nor I will go down as all-time all-stars, but we've earned jobs in the NBA and we've helped our teams win. How many guys can say as much?

In their early seasons as an NBA team, the Cleveland Cavaliers discovered, as have other teams founded through the expansion process, that victories are hard to come by. Players assembled from other teams, augmented by fresh rookies, take time to become accustomed to each other, and expansion teams usually lack the game-breaking superstar.

At that, the Cavaliers and their sister expansionists of the 1970–71 season, Portland and Buffalo, did their best, followed the percentages by attempting the right play at the right time, and, in due course, will reach relative equality through drafting, trading, and maturity. Should the Cavaliers contend for title status soon, guard Butch Beard, a 6-foot-3, 185-pound former Louisville U teammate of Wes Unseld, will be remembered as the man who played a major role. Originally drafted by Atlanta, Beard missed the 1970–71 season because of U.S. Army service, then returned to civilian life in 1971–72 to help the Cavaliers continue their climb from infancy to respectability. He was traded to Seattle in August 1972.

Butch Beard

Young teams can be minor tragedies in sports because they want so badly to win yet so often beat themselves. Players on a young team get to thinking so much it's an individual responsibility to turn a loser into a winner that they may try too hard sometimes, try to do a job and a half instead of just their own. Young teams also lose games because they fluster in critical moments—and I want to emphasize that there's a huge difference between flustering and *choking*. NBA players come from collegiate conference and national championship teams and are used to pressure. They don't choke. But remembering all the little details that go into pro victories is something players seem to learn only with patience.

I'm trying to say, if you've read between the lines, that Cleveland lost some games that they might have won with more experience—games the Cavaliers will win when they gain it. Even in 1971–72 we were *aware* of doing the right things at the right time, and more and more as the players mature together they're *doing* them, too.

I'm talking here about two special sets of situations in particular —protecting the ball in the closing seconds of each period to take best possible advantage of the 24-second clock, and taking into account the bonus-foul situations. Like so many others in pro ball, they're matters of making the percentage play at the percentage time. Even perfect execution doesn't guarantee a win, but you can try, anyway, to get as much going for you as the rules and pressures of a game allow.

Most fans are familiar with the percentage situation of trying to make sure you take the last shot attempt in each quarter. You try to gain what amounts to a 4-point edge by getting a last basket, but hitting it just before the buzzer sounds so that the team you're playing can't nullify it by taking the ball out, getting it up the floor, and scoring within the time remaining. What fans may not be familiar with is that the same percentage—thanks to the 24-second clock—can be carried a step further. We'll try to get a shot, say, with 33 or 34 seconds left in a period so that our opponent will have to take his shot within the 24-second limit and so that we'll then have the ball again for the last-gasper—two of the last three shots for us, in other words. Most coaches feel that the final shot ought to be taken with about 3 seconds left—too late for the other club to do anything with the ball if the shot is good, but permitting time for an offensive rebound attempt if it misses.

Coming down to the wire in periods when you know the other team has fouls to give, you try to have your best free-throw shooter handle the ball.

Experience comes in during these situations, because the team you're playing will sometimes hang back defensively from a man on your team who's not a good shooter, daring him to fire the ball so they'll get a chance to rebound. They also hope to have that man handle the ball, because they can gamble on fouling him and getting possession whether they're in the bonus yet or not. When a team plays the Lakers and the game is close coming down to the wire, it's almost automatic to try to foul Wilt Chamberlain when he gets the ball (even though you sort of feel guilty for putting so much extra pressure on a great star we all respect). We'd much rather take our chances with him at the free-throw line than see him muscle inside for a slam dunk, so the closest man to him will wrap his arms around him as quickly as he can after Wilt catches a pass.

The Lakers look for their opponents to be trying that strategy, so they make sure Wilt doesn't handle the ball. They give it to Jerry West or Gail Goodrich, and they'll even force your hand further by having all their other men move completely to the opposite side of the floor—what we call *clearing out*. Jerry is such a great one-on-one player, the Lakers are confident he'll either get a good percentage shot or be fouled, and he's justified their confidence so often in his career he's earned the nickname "Mr. Clutch."

The Cavaliers have that kind of player in Austin Carr, the great young guard from Notre Dame who was injured so much of his rookie season, but who has great talent. Spencer Heywood does it for Seattle, and I've taken my own chances with the ball, too—at Cleveland and at Seattle. Even though you play for a loser, you see, you can't get yourself to thinking like one.

8

A QUICK MIND IN A HEALTHY BODY—THAT HEALS FAST

A legend in his own time was a big, strong, slow, awkward, lovable giant from the Pacific Northwest who'd been a collegiate All-American and then gone into AAU ball, a blithe spirit whose fondness for basketball was exceeded only by his love for liquid refreshment of a punchy nature.

One early September night in this giant's home town—1960, it was —a sportswriter happened to visit a local pub popular among the region's athletes, ex-athletes, and sporting crowd. Our story's hero was sprawled all over the bar, obviously having spent considerable time there already that evening and obviously in jolly spirits, thanks to a considerable volume of beverage.

"Hey, John . . . hey, John," the jolly giant called out to the sportswriter as he entered the place. "I got shum marveloush newsh for you."

The newsman, intrigued and bemused, asked innocently, "What do you mean?"

"I been offered a job in pro basketball, and . . . and . . . and I gonna get two bonushes," gushed the ex-All-American.

"That's great," said the newsman, turning his nose quickly to avoid the aromatic exhaust of the giant's shouting. "But what do you mean, you're going to get two bonuses?"

"Lishen to thish . . . lishen to thish . . . I gonna get one bonush if I make the team," confided the ballplayer in a whisper which made up in loudness what it lacked in secrecy, "and I'm gonna get another bonush if I report in sh-sh-shape!"

It's said the Lord smiles warmly on drunks and little children, and, by golly, the fellow actually did report to the beckoning team, actually made the roster, actually played in the NBA for a couple of seasons. Did he get both his bonuses? It's not recorded.

The point here is that concern for physical condition is as old as athletics, but that acceptable standards change. The NBA today demands more in stamina, endurance, ability to withstand the grind of travel than ever before. Perennial front-runner in total playing time John Havlicek of the Boston Celtics, a former Ohio State All-American, emerges as the contemporary all-star best noted for his resistance to these draining factors of pro basketball life. Constantly the 6-foot-5 former "best sixth man in basketball" amazes his teammates and his rivals by seeming never to tire, no matter how tense the situation.

John Havlicek

The worst thing that can happen to a basketball player is to get tired. So he shouldn't get tired, even though he may have to run anywhere from six to eight miles during the course of a game, even though he may have to play tough defense, even though he may have to rebound and do other hard-work things too.

Not that the same thing would work for all athletes, but my personal choice and opinion for many, many years has been that avoiding fatigue is vital for me if I'm to be able to help my team—and help myself. Tired players, first of all, can't perform physically up to their capability, and, second, tired players seem to be much more vulnerable to getting seriously injured. "Fatigue makes cowards of us all," Vince Lombardi *always* lectured his football teams, and nothing that I've seen in basketball shows me that lesson isn't valid in my sport too. Running is my game.

If you're a truckdriver, you make sure when you report to work that the engine is in running order, that there's gas in the tank, and that there's plenty of oil. If you're an accountant, when you come to work you sharpen your pencils and haul out your notepads and percentage tables. If you're a basketball player, for the very same reasons, you make sure that *your* tools—your arms and legs, your muscles—are as ready as possible prior to every game.

I'm supposed to be a player who never gets tired, who hardly ever even raises a sweat. "That Havlicek is going to find out some-day what it is to be tired," my old teammate and ex-coach Bill Russell cackled in that unique laugh of his on a national telecast of an NBA game, "and he's just going to drop dead!" I admit it pleased me, because it was recognition that the year-round prepara-tions and precautions I take pay off in my ability to contribute to the Celtics' success and permit me to continue making my living as an athlete. I've been involved in sports ever since I was a little boy in Lansing, Ohio, and I have been fortunate all my life in being rather successful in about every sport I've tried. Whatever natural physical gifts I've been fortunate to have, I'd have wasted if I hadn't taken care to keep fit all the time, in season and out. I don't mean to sound like a goody-goody—I'm just explaining what's worked for one guy, a guy named Havlicek.

Keeping an athlete fit to perform is, I think, mostly his own responsibility, although it's partly his team's too. A good diet is a must, with an emphasis on proteins, salads, and vegetables, plenty of fruit juices and fluids. Athletes perspire heavily and must restore lost liquid. Perspiration also drains minerals and salts from their bodies, so athletes take salt tablets after games and practices to restore proper chemical balance and thus prevent leg cramps. The proper amount of rest is still another basic self-discipline thing that is an individual concern. I happen to feel my best, play my best with about eight hours of sleep each night, but I know other players who get by on five—and I know others who need nine or ten.

Probably the most important thing a basketball player can do to take care of himself physically is to pamper his feet. Basketball is a game of constant stops and starts, constant changes of direction, constant jumping. Your feet are always chafing one way or another inside your shoes, so most players take extra care to rinse their feet after every shower, following advice from their team trainers and doctors, to prevent "athlete's foot." Shoes should fit tightly enough so that chafing and friction are kept as slight as possible, but not so tight blood circulation is impaired. Basketball players can be ruined by blisters, and one way we avoid them is by wearing not just one pair of athletic socks, but two, of about 50 per cent wool, and we usually tape them at the tops to prevent chafing. Naturally, the

Tireless John Havlicek scoops a layup at the payoff end of a fast break.

NBA teams provide us with the best possible equipment, since players are valuable assets, but at other levels of ball, expenses are watched pretty carefully, and it's sometimes up to the young player to insist on shoes that give him good arch support, good inner-sole construction, and good traction. In case you ever have to buy your own shoes, or in case you ever decide to give someone a pair of sneakers as a gift, you generally wear a shoe one or one-half size smaller than your street shoes.

Next to your feet, literally as well as figuratively, your ankles are your greatest concern, and a must before every workout and game is to have your ankles wrapped or taped for additional support. Most coaches will fine a player, in fact, if he fails to get taped and then suffers a sprain. The quick stops and starts can punish you with twisted ankles, but a frequent cause of ankle injuries in basketball is that you come down from a jump and land on another guy's feet instead of on the floor. To get back to shoes for a moment, players mostly use low-cut shoes nowadays rather than old-fashioned high-cuts because they seem to be lighter, seem to give you a more streamlined feel. Because of the taping there's no difference in protection for your ankles one way or the other, and just a few players nowadays still wear the high-cuts. It's a matter of individual choice.

When a pro athlete is unlucky enough to get hurt, there's often a tough mental adjustment as well as a painful physical problem. Being healthy is sort of a point of pride for an athlete, a badge of honor. There's a fine line between being too proud to report a physical problem and going to the trainer for help so often you get accused of being a hypochondriac, but I think an athlete has to find that line for himself. My hope and intention personally are to keep healthy, keep fit, keep away from needing special attention from our trainer. But if I've got a twinge, a sniffle, or some other problem, I've got the professional responsibility of reporting it and getting treatment that'll keep me in the line-up.

Never get tired? It's a compliment that people say that about me, but I'll have to tell the world, here and now, that the man who can go from October to May, play 40 or more minutes a night, 82 regular season games a season, and then up to 21 playoff games without nearing exhaustion hasn't been born yet. All you can do is take the best precautions you can, really push yourself extra hard when there's a temptation to think about being tired, and keep your fingers crossed that when each game's crisis moment comes up you've got enough left physically to respond to it.

If perpetually-in-motion John Havlicek provides an example of general year-round fitness for his fellow pros and for flabby, cholesterol-plagued America in general, intense Lou Hudson of the Atlanta Hawks offers expertise in the mental and physical preparation a professional devotes to each night's specific game effort. The 6-foot-5 former University of Minnesota All-American has played both forward and guard for the Atlanta Hawks in a brilliant pro career, and, like Havlicek, he is one of the rare men in NBA annals to have earned all-star recognition at both positions.

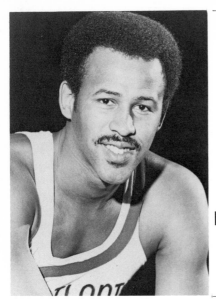

Lou Hudson

No matter what you've heard or read about the life of a pro basketball player, you can't grasp the way playing in the NBA grinds at you until you've gone through a season yourself. The sensation is like the special-effects technique in movies when they want to show the passage of time. The camera closes in on a calendar, and the pages turn slowly, then move faster and faster until they are a blur. In the NBA the early season games stand out in your memory, one at a time, but by Christmastime and into the new year the games seem to come at you one after another in the same kind of blur. At that, it's not the games piling up that drains you, it's the travel and the habits you fall into. It's a feeling, a drudgery you settle into, and by about February it seems that every time you look around you're either plodding down a long corridor from an airport passenger-loading area to the airplane or picking up your baggage in the lobby of a hotel to trudge once more up to your room. You feel you can keep going if you ride with the momentum of things, but if you sort of blink and look around, jolt yourself awake, you feel you've done exactly the same thing in exactly the same way a thousand times before.

No matter how deep a trance you go into, you have to be ready to go full speed in the games, prepared both physically and mentally, when time comes for the opening tip-off. It's the professional attitude you learn to adopt that keeps you going. Players who can't learn the self-discipline it takes for a player to keep chugging through an NBA season drop out. It's one of the things that separates the hot-shot college boy from a dependable NBA man.

Coaches feel that getting their players "up" for each game is one of their biggest, most difficult responsibilities. Still, I think it's an individual player's job to get himself thinking basketball and to get physically ready to play, even though some nights playing a basketball game is the last thing in the world you want to do. It's like any other job. Some mornings a man can hardly wait to get to his desk or his workbench, he's so eager to get going. Other days going to work is just an ordeal. The pro does his work no matter which mood he's in, and that's the way it has to be in the NBA too.

Mental preparation is the harder thing, made more difficult when you're playing away from home, because of travel. More often than not when you're on a road trip, you'll play four or five games in five or six nights, in a different city each night, and you'll fly from city to city either late at night after a game or early—sometimes very, very early—the next morning. Expansion of the league into seventeen cities now has meant shorter flights, but it also has created some brutal transportation problems. Or haven't you ever tried to get from Buffalo to Phoenix in the middle of winter? Remember, a pro basketball road party is only about sixteen or seventeen guys—the twelve players, the coach, the trainer, maybe a sportswriter or two. It's not like baseball or football, where fifty or sixty people are involved. You seldom fly charter, so you just about always have to rush to get to airports on time, and every man is responsible for his own luggage—usually a garment bag for your sports coats and suits; a smaller bag for your uniforms, shoes, sweat pants, and shirt and so forth; then your regular suitcase. The baseball and football guys just check in, and their gear is waiting for them in their hotel rooms. We basketball pros arrive at our hotels either very, very early in the morning or in early afternoon, lugging our stuff by ourselves. We usually will head for the coffee shop, for a sandwich or some other snack, and then go to our rooms to try to get some sleep. By midafternoon you start thinking about that night's game—who'll be guarding you, whom you'll be guarding, what happened the last time you played this team, what other match-ups are likely to be, what your team can or cannot do. You try to remember incidents between that team and yours, trouble between their players and yours—any thought that will help you get motivated, help get some adrenalin flowing as time comes to depart for the arena. I consider myself fortunate that, because of the kind of game I play, a finesse and *move* game rather than a muscling game, I can keep more or less calm and calculating. Some guys in the NBA try to get to where they're raging mad at the man they're going to match up against—a hate thing that can be ugly. You do what you have to do.

Physical preparation is more grinding routine, but easier to tolerate. Pros usually try to eat their biggest meal of the day, their pregamer, about four or five hours before tip-off time—about 3:30 or 4:00 P.M. This is another possible hassle for road games, because there aren't all that many restaurants ready to serve a decent meal that early. We get $19 per day in expense money—plenty on which to eat well if our timing were only better. A standard pregame meal with most players is steak, baked potato, salad, coffee or tea (not milk, because milk tends to build mucus in your mouth as you run), and maybe a scoop of ice cream or some pudding for dessert. In recent years some players have gone away from that kind of meal to pancakes or French toast—starchy kinds of meals, because the carbohydrates give quicker energy. Other pros—Gail Goodrich of the Lakers is one—find they play best on an all-purpose liquid meal like Sustagen or Metrecal and maybe some canned fruit.

Home or away, players start arriving at the arena around 90 minutes or so before the game. There's usually some mail waiting for you, and you go through it at your locker, bulling with the guys, maybe talking to a reporter who's asked for an interview, then heading for the training area to get your ankles taped. If you've been nursing an injury, you might arrive extra early for treatment. About an hour before the game, the locker rooms of most teams go off limits to anybody except the players, the coach, the assistant coach if the team has one (the Hawks have one, and a good one, in Gene Tormohlen), and the trainer. Now's the time to really start bearing down mentally, the time the coach will talk to you. Either before the coach talks to the club or afterward (some coaches skip meetings except for special problem times), players head for the johns to take care of—let's say "private bodily functions," to keep it polite. Twenty minutes or so before tip-off, you take a big extra breath, and everybody heads out the door. It's time to warm up.

Nobody works that hard physically during warm-ups, but the layup drills and jogging work loose the stiffness and the kinks, get the blood flowing through your muscles, stretch your ligaments and tendons. An athlete warms up slowly and thoroughly, because we're taught early in our careers that muscles and tendons are torn very easily and very, very painfully if a man tries to exert full strength too soon. Basketball teams will break up into individual-player shooting warm-ups after five minutes or so, and I make it a point to try the shots I'm going to use most often that night—from the corners on either side, from the top of the free-throw circle, 18 to 20 feet out on either side—the shots I've learned are my highest percentages. I dribble around just enough to get the feel of the ball, but most of the practice shots I take I try to take just as quickly as someone passes me the ball—without a dribble. On the Hawks, Pete Maravich is going to control the ball quite a bit of the time on offense, making the play and passing to the open man. Pete and I work well together in the backcourt because I move a lot without the ball, work into the open. I have the quick shot to use from outside, and when Pete gets the ball to me, I know exactly what to do with it. It's easy to see why I try the same kinds of shots in warm-ups I'll use in a game, and most pros follow the same habit. You always make sure to take some free throws too, and I'll also try to get another Hawk working with me—I'll shoot while he waves a hand in my face like a defensive man, then I'll do it while he shoots a few, so that we're sort of tuned up for what'll happen in the game.

Soon the two refs come out, the horn sounds to get the players off the floor, the lights dim, and the public-address announcer goes over the line-ups before they play the National Anthem. Then it's game time. Time to earn your money. You've psyched yourself to the point you're lean and mean and eager and ready. Run, man, shoot the ball, go after that rebound—you're a pro, man, and you have a job to do. Do it!

Some nights you win, some nights you lose. Pros learn not to get too happy, not too blue. Tomorrow will be another game, and pros know they'll have to go through the exact same process all over again. Blur. Montage. Life in the NBA. I am Lou Hudson. I play pro basketball. That says it all.

Human bodies—even those proportioned on a gigantic scale—are not built to withstand indefinitely the stresses and buffeting they are subjected to in the turmoil of a professional basketball game. The player who goes through an NBA season unhurt is the exception, not the rule, and one measure of a player's value to his team has become his ability to recover rapidly from an injury, ignore pain, yet still perform effectively.

Backcourt star Nate Archibald of the newly transferred (from Cincinnati) Kansas City team is a wiry-framed University of Texas at El Paso graduate who has become an all-star for his team, despite his not quite 6-foot height, because of his quickness, his aggressive, clever play, and his durability.

Nate Archibald

It's a good thing for pro basketball teams, talking money problems as they seem to do all the time, that they pay their trainers a set salary instead of so much for each inch of tape they wind around their players during a season. Trainers are probably as important to teams as their leading scorers, but paying them on a season-contract basis instead of per job makes them tremendous bargains. Every player in the NBA realizes that getting hurt is something that can happen at any time. The big thing is how bad any injury is, and then how long—if at all—an injury will keep a player on the sidelines. That's where the trainer comes in, because his knowledge and his work may mean the difference between an early return to action and a long, uncomfortable, unwanted vacation.

Joe Keefe is our trainer, and our players have learned to rely on him to give us the correct, immediate treatment to help keep pain down and also to start our bodies' healing processes as quickly as possible. Joe and the other trainers keep up all the time on research and developments in medicine, and whenever a new treatment is developed or a new device is introduced or a new healing drug discovered, they're right there to decide whether there's a way to use it to benefit athletes. An interesting thing is that, according to Joe and to some of the other trainers around the league, the more research that's done on medical aspects of sports, the more doctors learn about treating their regular, nonathlete patients too. Each team has an orthopedic surgeon "on call," and he'll attend every home game or have an associate of his on hand so he's available immediately to treat his own players or the other team's if something happens. The doctor and the trainer work very closely together every step of the way in an injury situation—from first, rush treatment to diagnosis to therapy to return to action. A player has to be willing to stand probably more pain than a normal person would have to stand with a similar injury, and a player also has to be willing to be completely honest with the trainer and the doctor if he's to get back in action in a hurry. Your coach wants you back as rapidly as possible, but coaches respect and seek the doctors' advice.

The pros regard injuries and recovering from them realistically. "Guts and tape!" has become just about as important a slogan in pro ball as "hit the open man" or "pass and cut." The thing to do is get whatever help the trainer can give you, then warm up well before a game, and play as hard as you can, as well as you can, as long as you can.

You want to play again as soon after a serious injury as you can, but you also have to do what the doctor and your trainer advise you to do, even if it means really going to the absolute limit of your individual pain threshold. You also have to realize that playing with an injury is empty, false heroics unless—after the best treatment and help your trainer can give you—you're a more effective player for your team, hurt, than the player from the bench who'd replace you. Even then, if playing with an injury is apt to aggravate it and prolong recovery time, you may have to be willing to keep idle so that you don't risk permanent disability which might end your career.

Since I was determined to make it in the NBA, even though I wasn't exactly what you'd call one of the most famous college players in my time, I figured out during my rookie year that the more I knew about my body and trainers' methods, the better I'd be able to handle being hurt and the better I'd be able to bounce back after injuries.

I learned that the first thing a trainer tries to do when he rushes out on the court to help a guy who's hurt is to figure, of course, what the injury is. Usually a player has gotten an elbow in his ribs or to his jaw, or slightly twisted an ankle or been poked or bumped accidentally some way or other. The shaken-up player may just need a moment or two to get himself together. Most trainers carry a pressurized container of liquefied ethyl chloride with them. They squirt it on a bruised or skinned spot, and the stuff hisses out as a very cold gas spray that sort of numbs the whole area. The spray helps you shake off the temporary pain, and you get right back into the flow of the game.

Other injuries don't let a player off that cheaply. The floor is hard, and we don't wear any padding in basketball. You can get hurt colliding with another player or by landing awkwardly in a fall or coming down from a jump, and you can snap tendons and ligaments all alone, maybe just straining too hard trying to break away for a solo layup. Invariably, if a trainer sees that an injury is more than something trivial, his first move will be to apply cold and pressure in order to keep down swelling. It was explained to me that part of the body's defense mechanism in an injury moment is to immobilize the damaged area. Blood vessels break, there's internal bleeding, and other fluids flood the area to prevent any movement. That's what swelling is, and mobility is exactly what the trainer will be trying to restore for you as soon as he can. Cold—either ice or chemical-compound cold packs—tend to minimize swelling, and therapy can't begin, usually, until the swelling begins to subside—maybe twenty-four to thirty-six hours later. Different players will react differently to the same injury, by the way. Some guys' ankles automatically balloon when they're sprained, yet other guys' ankles just puff a little. The amount of pain a person can tolerate—that threshold—also varies.

Players are X-rayed the same night they're hurt, if there's any doubt what the injury is, and the team doctor will determine whether there's a broken bone involved, tendon or ligament damage, a muscle tear, a dislocation, or whatever. Techniques of diagnosis improve all the time. A big advance in orthopedic medicine has been improved surgical techniques, and operations are performed maybe less than twenty-four hours after a player is injured if his team's doctor feels urgent surgery will speed and promote healing.

Fortunately only the most severe injuries require operations. Sprains and muscle pulls and tears are more common happenings, and the trainer takes advantage of the body's natural healing processes to speed his invalids back to full duty. You might say that using ice to prevent swelling is sort of fighting nature, but after that what a trainer is doing is attempting to speed up nature. Movement can't be back to normal until the dead blood cells released by hemorrhage and the other fluids are reabsorbed by the body, so the trainer will give you enzyme tablets—chemicals produced within your body naturally—to speed that process. Heat, whirlpool-bath treatments, ultra-sound waves, and old-fashioned hand massage all help increase blood circulation through an injured area and speed up the natural healing. The trainer will also use tape and elastic bandages and, if necessary, special braces or padding to protect an injured area. A common example of these is the heel padding a trainer will sometimes put in your shoe if you're coming back from a sprained ankle. Walking flatfooted is especially painful in a sprain because that puts extra stress on injured tissues, and the pain is your body's warning to you to be cautious. The padding lifts the foot, relieves the stress, and lets you be loose enough to play.

I've been fortunate so far that it hasn't happened to me, but I know of many, many times, on our team and other teams, when a trainer has worked on a player literally a full day—going from one thing to another and then back to the first treatment—to get a guy ready to play in a crucial game that night. If the game is important enough—a playoff, for instance—a doctor will desensitize an injury by giving a player injections of painkillers such as Novocaine or Xylocaine, and he may even give the player booster injections at halftime. I don't know of any coach who'll ask a doctor to resort to painkillers, however, no matter how big the game, if there's a danger of permanent, crippling damage. Doctors use similar caution in prescribing drugs, and use of either pep pills or "downers" among NBA players is uncommon.

You read all the time about professional athletes undergoing surgery, yet returning to action six week, eight weeks, a couple of months later. Players are as amazed at some of the quick recoveries as the public, believe me. I remember that I was still at school in El Paso in November of 1969 when Wilt Chamberlain of the Lakers suffered a torn tendon in his right knee going up uncontested for a slam dunk against Phoenix. The next day I remember reading that he was going to undergo immediate surgery, that he'd be out at least for the rest of the season, and that maybe he'd never play again. By mid-March—and I remember how amazed I was—he was back in the line-up, and I recall that he and Jerry West and Elgin Baylor had an especially hot playoff. They took the Lakers all the way to the seventh game of the NBA finals before they lost the world championship to the Knicks.

After I turned pro myself the next year, I had a chance once to talk to Wilt about how he'd had such an amazing recovery. He told me that he'd never worked so hard in his life as he had coming back from that surgery. When I talked over what Wilt told me with the Lakers' trainer, Frank O'Neill, and with Joe Keefe, they both pointed out to me that speed in recovery is far more important for an athlete than for someone in another profession, that an athlete will be asked to work harder, longer, more often, and with more pain in coming back from a major injury than other people. Of course, it's up to a player to decide if he's willing to do the work and stand the pain. If he agrees, he's likely to be a contributing team member again in a hurry. That means money in the bank for him and for his team.

Wilt told me that his injured leg's thigh and calf muscles lost three to five inches around while the full-length cast was in place after the surgery. He began whirlpool therapy, swimming, and lifting weights every single day of the week to get himself back in shape to play as soon as the cast was removed. When his leg got strong enough, he began doing miles of roadwork on the beach near Santa Monica and Malibu, and he even took up the strenuous game of volleyball—they play it on the beach on the West Coast, and they tell me that the running and jumping in the sand is really exhausting. Getting his timing and smoothness back and working back in with the rest of the Lakers was a second major set of problems once he rejoined the team, Wilt said, but things smoothed out in due time, and he had the satisfaction of proving he was eager to help his team, willing to do all that work even though it would have been perfectly reasonable by most medical standards for him to have delayed until the following September before coming back.

If Wilt had been, say, an insurance agent or an investment counselor when he got hurt instead of an all-pro pivot man, he could have gone for therapy three times a week instead of seven, lifted weights a couple of afternoons a week instead of every day—

and lifted lighter loads, at that. The therapy process would have been similar, but not nearly as concentrated as is necessary for athletes.

I've been fortunate up to·now to have had just my normal share of temporary physical problems—a few pulls, a few sprains, a usual season's quota of floor burns and scratched knees from scrambling after loose balls. I've avoided broken bones or ruined knees up to now, and I hope I can keep avoiding them. To play in the NBA is to take that chance. All I can say is that if I get hurt I'll be glad Joe Keefe is running out to take care of me and that I hope I'll have the kind of guts Wilt showed so that I'll be able to grit my teeth, bear down, do whatever Joe tells me to, and get back in uniform quickly. I've already gone through a lot to become a player in the NBA, and I wouldn't want to blow it by being either lazy or overly sensitive to a little pain.

9

HOW TO BECOME A SUPERFAN

It's a crushing burden to be a convert, no matter what it is you've been converted to.

In my case the change was from typical Southern California sports fan, circa 1960, to wild-eyed pro basketball enthusiast, circa 1960¾. I've been an evangelist for pro basketball ever since. Like all converts, I'm not just an enthusiastic, 100-per-cent devotee. I'm a zealous, 200-per-cent advocate, determined that the enjoyments and gratifications I've savored through the years be shared by all my fellow mortals. At that, mere sharing of enthusiasm hasn't been enough. No, I've been determined that not only my enthusiasms be shared, but my reasons for them too.

As a boy, I played playground softball and, later, true baseball, switched to touch football in the fall, and returned to baseball following each pre-Thanksgiving-weekend UCLA-USC titanic and the close of league action by the Rams. Basketball was a tolerated game, to be played only when teachers insisted during physical-education period in school. Baseball's subtleties and football's muscular, militaristic strategems were easy for a boy to grasp, but basketball was too difficult—especially for a Southern Californian, considering that the sport offered him no popular heroes to worship as he could Bob Feller, Joe DiMaggio, Ted Williams, Bob Waterfield, Norm Van Brocklin, Crazylegs Hirsch, and the others.

Interest in sports led to interest in talking and writing about them —next best thing to being an athlete, you see. By high school I was determined to become a sportswriter and pursued a course of intense study and good fortune which led, by 1960, to a role as an assistant editor and sometime writer for the sports staff of the no longer extant Los Angeles *Examiner.*

Southern California's first decent showcase for basketball—the Los Angeles Memorial Sports Arena—had been built the year before, and it became haven for UCLA and USC as well as for a few pro games by visiting teams from the far-off National Basketball Association. Basketball had its hard little core of fans in Southern California before the Sports Arena was built, but only afterward could the sport start to make the inroads into the public imagination it had made elsewhere in the United States decades before. In the spring of 1960 the Minneapolis Lakers were transferred to Los Angeles. In October of that year, for a preseason exhibition contest against the world-champion Boston Celtics, I was invited to join the Lakers' traveling party on the 160-mile bus trip to and from the team's Sports Arena offices in Los Angeles and Swing Auditorium in San Bernardino.

That bus ride was the hook that converted a casually interested basketball neutral into a fierce advocate, and it was the fascination of meeting the Lakers as individual personalities, before I spent extensive time watching them actually on the playing floor, that did it. I was introduced to Elgin Baylor that afternoon, having seen him play in games only twice while I was still too unlearned about the game to appreciate his full, incredible magic. I knew people, however, and his magnetism, wit, and leadership of the team, his loud jeering and bantering with his teammates in the way of the professional athlete was marvelous fun. I became a fan of Elgin Baylor the blithe spirit and dominating personality well before I became a fan of Elgin Baylor the unstoppable basketball dervish. Jerry West, a silent rookie from West Virginia, was on the bus ride too, along with grinning, puckish Rudy LaRusso, Baylor's off-court verbal and argumentative straight man just as he was a powerful 6-foot-7 forecourt aide in games; and irreverent, hip Hot Rod Hundley. After a budding career of interviewing well-meaning, but frequently dull, baseball and football stars, the Lakers were a revelation for me. I had the good fortune in the next few months to meet players of other teams too, and found them great company as individuals as well as brilliant athletes in games. I've covered Laker games for newspapers and magazines ever since, and my enthusiasm has never wavered.

Thus I was converted to pro basketball by its people—it's front-office manipulators as well as its fun practitioners—before I began to learn the tactical intricacies of the game. My testimony is that, for one man at least, appreciation of the game has been heightened by recognizing the personalities first—with all their human foibles— and only later by digging into the philosophy of the fast break or the full-court press. I found that knowledge of the latter increased my appreciation of the former, and that has been my underlying intention in this book. In our attempt to explain underlying principles of the NBA style of play, players and I have purposely expressed generalities and talked in terms of *ideal* plays or situations. Points of tactics or techniques have been reduced to specific detail to convey ideas intended to help young players, but also to provide insight for all fans into the things that are acting, reacting, and interreacting within a pro basketball game at all times.

If ideal situations existed every night for every NBA game, it would be possible to predict with absolute accuracy, as soon as the NBA schedule was announced each summer, exactly how many games each team would win or lose, the order in which they would finish, and the results of postseason playoffs. Kareem Abdul-Jabbar has an *on-paper* advantage over every other center in the NBA, and therefore he ought to dominate his man every game. Spencer Haywood is the most powerful forward in the league, so theoretically he should never be defensible on a move to the basket. The Lakers have dominating Wilt Chamberlain and crisis-proof Jerry West, and they should never lose a game—except, possibly, to Milwaukee—in an ideal situation.

Reality and experience show that the ideal occurs only once in a while, though. Fatigue affects games; players are subject to moods; some men become emotionally propelled against some opponents, remain sluggish against others. Travel conditions and injuries and personal problems and a thousand and ten other things prevent teams from meeting at the mythical ideal night after night, and thus there is a constant uncertainty and perpetual fascination in pro basketball. The better team and the better man do not always prevail, and how sweet this truth is for those of us aware that the NBA consists of a group of *people* who play a difficult game, not a group of personalityless robots who make the difficult look simple through more-than-human capability.

There is great temptation to say, "The most important thing in watching a pro basketball game is . . ." and then to list a single

In a one-on-one battle of great centers, Nate Thurmond soars past Willis Reed for a layup. (*Courtesy of Ron Koch.*)

facet of the game. This would be ultimate generalization and ultimate inaccuracy, because an observation based on a decade of
studying the NBA is that no one factor determines outcomes of all
games, but that, instead, there are many dynamics at work in any
particular game, that one often emerges as the most telling on a
given night. Rebounding strength probably has the greatest influence
on whether teams win or lose, but unusually good or unusually
poor shooting may be the most significant factor some nights, and
at other times the winner will be the team that played exceptionally
aggressive defense.

It is impossible, in watching pro basketball, to learn too much
about individual players or too much about entire teams. Each
player has his individual style, his favorite shots and favorite
shooting locations on the floor, an individual preference for a particular aspect of the game, personalized ways of doing things. When
a dozen individual styles are blended within a team and then
influenced by the commands of a coach with his own views of
how the game should be played, an over-all *team style* emerges.
The fan who studies first the players on his favorite team, then
players on all the other teams, eventually begins to grasp personal
differences among players as well as the subtle differences among
team outlooks. Knowledge of what individuals and teams usually
want to do in games provides the foundation for enlightened NBA-
watching, and to that knowledge in time will be added (with
whatever diligence or speed seems to provide the most personal
satisfaction) grasp of such dynamics as teams' quests for momentum,
attempts to thwart opponents' momentum, failure to move without
the ball, careless defense, and other night-to-night factors.

The "superfan" creates a mental image, prior to every game, of
the individual as well as team styles that will be interreacting in
the evening's combat, keeps in mind underlying philosophies of
basketball, and then watches the game unfold to determine whether
things are happening which vary from what he had reason to
expect, and if so, how. The variation—which might be caused by
injury, laziness, special motivation, individual or team foul situations, unusually good or bad rebounding or any of a number of
factors—is the significant thing that particular night, the aspect of
pro basketball to be written about by sportswriters in their reports
on the game or talked about by a superfan and his friends after the

game. One generality it seems safe to make, in other words, is that knowing the *usual* is a requirement for recognizing the *unusual*.

Among the dynamics that affect a game's outcome is tempo. Some teams play best at a helter-skelter pace, some at a more methodical speed. A Boston Celtics fan might approach a game between his team and, say, the Chicago Bulls by considering that the Celtics fast break at every opportunity, while the Bulls prefer a deliberate, more cautious tempo. The fan knows that rebounding controls the tempo of a game, and knows that Boston has a slim "probable" advantage on the boards over the Bulls, while Chicago is probably the better team defensively. As the first quarter unfolds, the fan might gauge whether the Bulls are getting a "normal" share of defensive rebounds and are playing at their preferred speed or whether the Celtics are getting easy baskets by grabbing the ball often, throwing the quick outlet pass, and getting high-percentage shots and layups off their break. The fun of being superfan comes from the occasional game in which teams veer from the norm—should Boston decide to slow things down or Chicago speed things up, should Chicago play uncharacteristically poor defense or should the Celtics find getting rebounds suddenly difficult. Detroit has long been a team that prefers outside shooting to a driving game. Baltimore (with Wes Unseld) stresses the fast break. New York sets lots of picks and screens outside. And other teams have their own characteristics.

Watching special match-ups has been a favorite occupation of pro basketball fans for years, and so it ought to be. Jerry West matching up against Oscar Robertson when the Lakers play the Bucks is a fascinating game-within-a-game. When Unseld comes up against Nate Thurmond in a duel of outstanding centers, fireworks erupt. When Dave DeBusschere matches muscle and determination against the improvisations and improbable swoops and moves of Connie Hawkins, the drama is intense. The superfan savors and anticipates these special match-ups—but he watches to see the variations, too. In 1970 the Lakers played the New York Knicks in a historic world-championship series which the Knicks finally won in a seventh game played before nearly twenty thousand screaming fans at Madison Square Garden. Television viewers throughout the nation thrilled as Willis Reed fought back the pain of a horribly torn thigh muscle and inspired the Knicks to victory, but the superfan enjoyed additional insight into the outcome by noting that coach Red Holzman had made a major gamble after the second game of the series. He took Walt Frazier, clearly his best defensive guard, off Jerry West and assigned him instead to rookie Dick Garrett, while veteran Dick Barnett, an ex-Laker considered by most people to be strictly a backcourt offensive gunner, was asked to contain the Laker superstar. Holzman explained later that the Knicks' offense had been sluggish, that he felt Frazier could make more of a playmaking and shooting contribution freed from the problem of attempting to shackle West. Further, the cagey New Yorker explained, Barnett was an underrated player defensively and he'd thought (correctly, as it turned out) Frazier's ball-hawking tactics might be more effective pitted against a rookie playing in his first pro showdown series than against a proven, clutch-play-specializing veteran like West. The switch in defensive assignments didn't decide the series in the Knicks' favor, but it played a significant part in their win, and those reporters and fans who noted the change early, who considered why it had been made, and later heard Holzman explain his thinking, were far ahead in fun and knowledge over less knowledgeable observers. In the 1971–72 title series between the clubs, West was in a shooting slump; Frazier guarded him, but starred offensively too.

Just as much to be considered is the game situation in which a team makes a drastic departure from its normal pattern of play in order to balance a tendency or talent of a rival. Another NBA championship playoff, between Los Angeles and Boston in 1967, hinged largely on a situation of this type. Los Angeles had won the regular season Western Division championship, using 6-foot-5 Elgin Baylor and 6-foot-7 Rudy LaRusso as starting forwards, 6-foot-11 LeRoy Ellis at center, 6-foot-3 West and 6-foot-2 Walt Hazzard as regular guards. Six-foot-8 Bob Boozer had had a fine season as number-three forward, and 6-foot-2 Jim King and then rookie Gail Goodrich, 6 feet even, contributed to an unusually deep—if physically small—set of guards. John Havlicek had been devastating against the Lakers all that season—too quick at 6-foot-5 for the Lakers' bigger forwards to handle consistently, too big and strong for any of the Lakers' guards except West when he swung to a backcourt position. Approaching the playoffs, it seemed Havlicek would be spending most of his playing time at forward, since the Celtics were physically hurting up front, but had K. C. Jones, Sam Jones, and Larry Siegfried ready to go at guard. As Game No. 1

unfolded—on a Sunday afternoon at Boston Garden to open Red Auerbach's final series as Celtics coach—the Lakers fell behind as Havlicek, predictably, swerved around LaRusso, Baylor, and Boozer for telling points. Fred Schaus was still coaching the Lakers, and he gambled daringly by moving his all-pro guard, West, up to forward to combat Havlicek, at the same time inserting King and rookie Goodrich as his guards. The combination clicked, and the Lakers emerged the opening-game winner in overtime, 133 to 129. Schaus stayed with that basic combination the rest of the series, and the Lakers just missed what would have been their first world championship when Boston scored a 95–93 victory on its home court in game number seven. The Lakers' three-guard alignment neutralized much of Havlicek's special effectiveness, but it was a strain for West and the others, a change from what had been proved most effective for them all season. Well as the Lakers played, Bill Russell was dominating as usual, and they couldn't pull off the upset. The triple-guard line-up became another sad entry in the Lakers' log of playoff frustrations, an example of the advantage maintained by an initiating team over a team reacting to another's initiative.

It's common knowledge in the NBA, to cite another "key" to look for in games, that Kareem Abdul-Jabbar prefers to set up at low post, on the left of the key, so that he can swing toward the basket and use his incredibly effective right-handed, downward-sweeping hook shot from virtually point-blank range. A Milwaukee game's decisive factor any given night is whether the opposing center is able to muscle Jabbar away from his favorite position, force him either to shoot from farther out than he prefers normally or to resort to other shots altogether. Wilt Chamberlain relies on another tactic against Jabbar—conceding the shot to him to greater degree than any other center, but then leaping right with the younger, taller ex-UCLA star to attempt to block. The lesson for the superfan: Watch Jabbar's hook shot or whether he's forced to hook left-handed, take his jumper facing the basket, or not be able to shoot at all. Against the Lakers, watch whether Wilt's unorthodox defensive tactic seems to be effective, and also watch to see what defensive problems Wilt creates for Jabbar at the other end of the floor.

The generation of shot-blocking centers which began with Bill Russell and Chamberlain, and which now seems to be becoming the rule rather than the exception among NBA teams, has created another ploy-and-counterploy situation which is an important part of many games. Shot-blocking, rebound-concentrating centers such as Chamberlain, Jabbar, Nate Thurmond, Elmore Smith, or Elvin Hayes are generally most effective if they're able to remain near the basket defensively. In that deep area they're often able to leave their assigned men and reach out to block shots of rival players who have eluded their defenders and are daring enough to encroach upon Big Man's Land. They shut off the opposition's driving game and they're also closer to the backboard for rebounds. Figuring the appropriate counterstrategy is simple; making the strategy work is something else. If the defensive center wants to remain near the basket, he'll have to permit the offensive center wide-open shooting room outside. The superfan watches when, for example, the Golden State Warriors play Detroit. The Warriors' Thurmond prefers to hang back, blocking shots and in position to rebound; Detroit's Bob Lanier is a brilliant outside shooter. If Lanier makes shot after shot from 15 to 20 feet away while Thurmond lays off him, Golden State will have to decide eventually whether (1) to continue permitting those shots while Thurmond shuts off everything else or (2) whether to have Nate the Great attempt to crowd Lanier. On the other hand, if Lanier is only moderately accurate from outside while Thurmond comes to dominate the inside area and the rebounding, Detroit will have to consider a change.

The possible variations on the will-he-go-outside-or-won't-he game are fascinating. A team with a shot-blocking, rebound-grabbing center, but with no big forwards, can be walloped badly on nights it must send its big man out to the perimeter for one-on-one defense, and so retains little rebounding strength inside. Strong, rebound-conscious forwards such as John Block of Philadelphia, Clyde Lee of Golden State, Happy Hairston of the Lakers, or Curtis Rowe of Detroit increase in value to their teams at such times.

Another type of individual variation to watch for is whether a particular player seems to be doing what he's noted for, or is instead departing from habit and working at something different.

Walt Frazier, to name one player, usually looks for ball-stealing opportunities throughout a game. If he plays a more orthodox defense on a particular night, it's a variation from the normal, and the next question is why. Whereas fans and reporters have no particular advantage over each other *during* games, the news-media

Aggressive Archie Clark begins a drive to the basket by slicing past his defender. (*Courtesy of Martin Blumenthal.*)

members have a big edge afterward, because reporters are permitted inside the locker rooms to ask questions. "You didn't try for many steals tonight guarding Dave Bing," Frazier might be asked after a game against Detroit. "Why was that?" And Frazier might reply, "I have a pulled thigh muscle and didn't want to gamble." Or he might say, "Bing is too clever with the ball. Coach Holzman didn't want me to take the chance." Or he might have still other reasons. The point is that, for some reason, he failed to play what has become his "expectable" game. On nights Pete Maravich is missing from outside, he'll resort more often to the drive, to give another example.

Preparation is the best way to avoid mistakes, for players and for reporters and fans. To get maximum entertainment value from the money he pays for his ticket, a fan does well to do his "homework" just as thoroughly as a player does his. The fan who takes his seat without prior awareness of injury situations on both teams, without considering the effect that night's game may have on the standings, without considering whether either team is on a winning or losing streak, is restricting his enjoyment to the obvious, momentary things that take place before him. The superfan, armed with pregame thought about possible individual match-ups, aware of the standings, familiar with the over-all "personalities" of the two teams, and also of some of the characteristics of individual players, not only enjoys games more deeply than his casual-arriving brethren, he also enjoys them longer. Casual fans are entertained for two hours of elapsed time, but the superfan enjoys games hours in advance of tip-off time, hours afterward.

Second-guessing coaches is as much a sports fan's birthright in America as his right to vote, but it's not nearly as much fun, I've found, to be critical of a coach in uninformed ways as it is to keep right up with him mentally from opening tip-off to final buzzer.

First, consider tempo and pattern of the game in its opening moments. Does either team seem to be taking swift command? The coach of a team hit by an opponent's sudden hot streak ought to look for a break in the momentum, and it is fun for the fan— unless he's so partisan his team's sudden jeopardy makes him lose the ability to consider things coolly—to decide along with the coach when and whether to call a time out. Another way to think along with the coach is to study each offensive-defensive and defensive-offensive match-up. The coach attempts to exploit any advantage that seems to be opening to his team—the opponent who may be injured and, that night, half a step slow, the unexpected line-up change that forces a rookie to guard a veteran or vice versa, or the player, on either team, in early foul trouble.

Coaches know their own personnel as well as their opponents' and attempt to anticipate, like chess rivals, what a countermeasure might be to any move they make. Roy Rubin of Philadelphia has 7-foot Mel Counts available to him if he wishes to attempt to create a corner mismatch, for instance, but he may resist using Counts against Atlanta because he anticipates his rival coach may use Lou Hudson at forward and have the smaller man try to run Counts into the floor. Rubin might also refrain from using Counts as a game-changer against Los Angeles because Bill Sharman might counter the substitution with 6-foot-11 LeRoy Ellis. Fans may consider exactly the same possibilities, be prepared for possible substitutions, and then judge whether they succeed or flop. There's fun to be had in the anticipation, even more fun in the satisfaction of having been smart enough to anticipate correctly.

Forgive the "200-per-center," the convert to pro basketball, if he seems to ramble on about all the possible combinations of circumstances which, he claims, bear upon a game's outcome. No excuses. It's just that kind of sport, endlessly varied and infinitely entertaining because it combines so much physical skill with so much mental anguish. There are no bad pro basketball games. Some may be better than others, but seldom is one of them boring.

Pro basketball has to be fun for its players and its followers, or something is wrong. Winning teams recognize this easily, for winning is the most fun thing of all. Losers forget the enjoyment to be had, become trapped on a treadmill of too much thinking, too much strategizing, not enough simple joy at doing their difficult things well. It is a dangerous temptation, too, for spectators to become so wrapped up in theoretical and technical considerations of NBA play that they lose the ability to appreciate the whimsical and trivial. Details of technique are worth knowing only insofar as spectators gain appreciation that the larger-than-life giants who perform in the glare of public attention are thinking, feeling, laughing, crying men first, examples of athletic perfection only on occasion, and unfeeling machines never. Know *why* strategy decrees that players do or don't do certain things, but please never become so concerned about the mechanics of a play that you forget the humanity of the man who attempts it.

I don't think it matters all that much, really, that Jerry West jumps straight up and keeps his elbow tucked underneath his hand trying to score from 22 feet away with 2 seconds left in a tie game. More wonderful by far than the mechanics of basketball is the coolness with which the superstar ignores his anxieties, exposes himself to accusations of failure, and dares accept the burden of victory or defeat.